MW00719740

TESTIMONIALS

"My heart resonates with the vision and ministry of The Widow's Project. In my past work as an overseer of ministers and churches, and in my present work as a pastoral counselor, helping others deal with transition and change is crucial. Never are the issues related to transition and change any more intrusive than when we lose a spouse. It is no wonder that God has called His Church to minister specifically to the needs of widows and widowers in our faith communities. The Widow's Project is leading the way in this powerful demonstration of God's agape' love care."

Rev. Leslie E. Welk, MA, Pastoral Counselor and Executive Vice President, Ministry Resources International, Former Superintendent of the Northwest Ministry Network Assemblies of God

"The Father heart of God burns with lovingkindness to all, especially towards those who live in the struggles of powerlessness and loneliness. He has invited his people to care with Him about others gripped in these realities, articulating things like, 'And what does the Lord require of you? To act justly and to love mercy and to walk humbly with your God,' (Micah 6:8) and, 'Religion that God our Father accepts as pure and faultless is this: to look after orphans and widows in their distress...' (James 1:27). The Widows Project steps into a much needed area of concern and practical care, aiding the people of God to do the works of God."

Chris Manginelli, Senior Pastor, Mill Creek Foursquare, Lynnwood, WA.

"It is with joy I share my thoughts on Rolland Wrights vision "The Widows Project". This area of service that is mandated by God himself is one of the most neglected areas of service in what is called church throughout our cities and the world. James tells us: Pure religion and undefiled before God and the Father is this, To visit the fatherless and widows in their affliction, and to keep himself unspotted from

the world (James 1:27). In Paul's letter to Timothy he devotes a large part of his letter to instructing the church on how to properly conduct ministry to widows. In the Law of Moses, we are instructed that we can either be blessed or even cursed by God as He watches how we treat widows.

"Yet in 36 years of ministry I have never seen the likes of what the Lord has shown Rolland to do through the widow's project. He has seen the God mandate that this area of service must be restored to action within the church. The Widows Project is a vision to network globally and locally by networking widows to quality resources and the resources of Christian businesses and ministries to the widows that need them. I praise our God for such a ministry as this returning to the Lords church and encourage you to prayerfully consider what part & role you may have in this work! God Bless!"

Apostle Steven Anderson, Answer the Call Ministries & The Alliance for Christian Unity

May the reading of this book "compell" you to serve + engage with

THE WIDOWS PROJECT

SERVING THE WIDOWED WITH THE FATHER'S HEART

Rolland

BY

ROLLAND WRIGHT

© 2017 – 2019 by Rolland Wright. All rights reserved. No part of this book may be transmitted or reproduced in any form, or by any means, mechanical or electronic, including photocopying, without written permission of Rolland Wright.

ALL RIGHTS RESERVED. This book contains material protected under International and Federal Laws and Treaties. Any unauthorized reprint or use of this material is prohibited. No portion of this book may be used, reproduced, stored in a retrieval system, or transmitted in any form or by any means — electronic, mechanical, photocopy, recording, scanning, or other — without express written permission from the authors or publisher, except for brief quotation in critical reviews or articles. It is illegal to copy this book, post it to a website, or distribute it by any other means without permission from the authors and publisher.

Published by
The Widows Project
The Mail Room -- 3616 Colby Ave. #788, Everett, WA 98201
Phone: 844-494-3697
Website: www.thewidowsproject.org
Email: rolland@thewidowsproject.org

Copyright Use and Public Information
Unless otherwise noted, images have been used according to public information laws.
ISBN: 978-0-578-61110-5 Paperback

Limits of Liability and Disclaimer of Warranty The author and publisher shall not be liable for the reader's misuse of this material. This book is for strictly informational and educational purposes.

Scripture quotations taken from the New American Standard Bible® (NASB),
Copyright © 1960, 1962, 1963, 1968, 1971, 1972, 1973,
1975, 1977, 1995 by The Lockman Foundation
Used by permission. www.Lockman.org

Scripture taken from the Tree of Life version
© 2015 by the Messianic Jewish Family Bible Society.
Used by permission of the Messianic Jewish Family Bible Society.
"TLV" and "Tree of Life Version" and "Tree of Life Holy Scriptures" are trademarks registered in the United States Patent and Trademark office by the Messianic Family Bible Society.

Disclaimer

The views expressed are those of the author and do not reflect the official policy or position of the publisher or The Widows Project This publication is designed to provide accurate and authoritative information regarding the subject matter covered. It is sold with the understanding that the publisher is not engaged in rendering legal, accounting, clinical or other professional advice. If legal advice or other expert assistance is required, the services of a competent professional should be sought. The opinions expressed by the authors in this book are not endorsed by The Widows Project, and are the sole responsibility of the author rendering the opinion.

ACKNOWLEDGEMENTS

It is a daunting but rewarding task to consider founding an organization like The Widows Project, and it is nice to see all the planning culminate into a launch date. It feels like the anticipation that we parents have when our child is about to take his or her first steps. We are proud for them, for their first accomplishments.

A number of people have been central in bringing The Widows Project alive. The first person that I shared my vision with, and has been supremely supportive throughout the process, is my friend Bill Morris. We met some 14 years ago under similar circumstances and have remained good friends even though geographically separated. We pray for each other and share our love for sports (even though we cheer opposing teams), along with our appreciation for the Christian music icons of our generation. I am grateful for his continued friendship, encouragement, support, and website skills.

Every team needs assistant coaches, and every business or organization needs a mentor. When I have had the opportunity to speak, I have shared my conviction of God's providence and His serendipity (God-planned appointments, GPAs) and related a few key experiences throughout my life.

Every once in a while, someone comes into your life and stays for longer than a day or a week, hopefully a lifetime. There has been a confident assurance throughout this process that all the resources (in people) were available to me. Some I had known for years, like John Griffith and our common love for slow pitch softball. In younger years we competed against each other's teams, and then in later years, to my pleasure, we were teammates. He is a quiet, steady friend!

Then I met Rick McGregor at a Bible study, and our lives gravitated together. Rick has provided great counsel from his expertise and friendship (even though we again cheer for opposing college teams) in worshipping together and on the tennis court. Both John and Rick formed my original board, and I appreciate them greatly. I consider both of these men serendipities—along with the man that took our rawness and helped me to put a vision into words, and then synthesized that information into a vision and mission statements.

I met Paul's wife Nancy first, as I was referred to her because she had previously led a grief support group at Mill Creek Foursquare Church (MC4S) in Lynnwood, Washington. It was through her that I became aware of the Grief Share organization. A brief time later, I discovered that Paul was involved with my alma mater's fundraising campaign, and I accompanied Nancy and Paul to one of the campaign events. I smile now, amazed at the kingdom resources that God put together purposely, not accidentally. I thank them both for being "available" and sharing their wealth of resources for the kingdom.

I also want to thank those that were so gracious in sharing information with me about starting a nonprofit organization, and creating our bylaws and meeting requirements for 501c3 tax exemption. People like Todd McNeal with Hand in Hand; with Pregnancy Resource Center; Sylvia Anderson with Everett Gospel Mission; Jon Siegel with Dignity Memorial; Doug Clark with CRU; and Paul Kennell with VIVA network North America.

Then more GPAs appeared in the mailroom of all places. Our organizational photographer, Rafael Estrada (who lives more than an hour away) and Eileen Howard (a widow from Vermont, here caring for her 98-year-old mother, who is also a widow) both were met in the Mail Room.

On LinkedIn, I met Di Patterson, America's Gerontologist; and also, Mary Salamon, publisher and writer for Marysville Tulalip Life Magazine in Everett, Washington. Both have become incredible resources for

TWP. Through Rick and John I have met Kat Foley, who has benevolently shouldered the birthing of this book and added a needed touch with the English language; Curt Shriner, owner of the Historic Everett Theatre, who graciously made this venue available for our first Christmas Benefit Concert; Bayard Dubois, Director of Breath of Aire for providing the 'air' to lift TWP and helping us launch our services to Snohomish County; John Dammarell and Liberty Road Foundation for their support and introducing me to Draw the Circle; and Robin Horne, numerous sacrificial hours editing; Dave Sproul and District 4 Creative (www.district4creative.com), video that creates the message.

What an amazing team that God has surrounded me with.

I want to thank the numerous intercessors that have prayed us through and now are praying us beyond. You know who you are, and I ask you to pray even more fervently (Acts 12:5) for us. You are appreciated more than I can express.

There will be more serendipities and more testimonies of God's providence as the years go by. The story of The Widows Project is not complete—and never will be—because we are a living organization that is ever growing. We will always be seeking the planned appointments that He has for you and us. To that end, God bless.

TABLE OF CONTENTS

FOREWORD

When I landed with a thud in the place of widowhood in 2013 it felt as if no one had ever experienced the kind of emotional pain I was grappling with in those initial months. How can a woman in her early 50's kiss her husband goodbye in the morning and by that night be faced with doing life solo? As the fog began to clear I realized that this was not an experience unique to me. If you are fortunate you come into meaningful contact with other widows. Those interactions open your eyes to some similar emotions, anxieties and longings that widows navigate on their grief journey. But what if you are given the opportunity to meet a man whose words, actions and prayer life are passionately directed towards ministering to the widow and widower?

Surely, he must be a widower, right?

As I have dialogued with people about The Widows Project, they can understand why I as a widow have engaged with the organization, however inevitably one of their questions is 'so if the founder is not a widower why is he doing this?'

This book helps to answer that very valid question.

Once you have received an answer to that question through the reading of these pages you will tumble into the frosting on the cake at the end. A 21-Day devotional. Any support system for a widow is important but ultimately it is time in the presence of God which will be your strength. God's Word and presence is available 24/7 which is particularly comforting in those middle of the night hours when a widow just cannot seem to sleep.

Do you wonder if God deeply cares for widows? Rolland as he highlights widows in the Scripture points out Mary the mother of Jesus was also a widow. Think about what transpired at the foot of the cross between Jesus and John. Yes, Jesus cared for widows in his time of most intense suffering.

We are called to be Christ followers, to be Christ like. This book is a clarion call to action. To embrace practical compassion for surviving spouses. This is not a one man calling - but a mandate to the church.

I challenge you to read with an open heart.

Discover if the same conviction that gripped Rolland's heart ' when and where have I dismissed or ignored the widow or widower?' begins to stir your heart also.

Best,
Deanna Rode
Mentorship Director & Director of Side by Side Seminars

CHAPTER 1

CAN YOU IMAGINE?

The vision statement for The Widows Project (TWP) is to uniquely serve widows and widowers with the love of Jesus.

In and of itself, it seems a simple statement. Yet to successfully accomplish this task, it is going to take a lot of leadership and partnerships with churches, local organizations, small businesses, major corporations, national organizations, a good executive board, quality staffing, effective use of our website and social media, and many volunteers.

In the following paragraphs, I hope to project an image of what this would look like. Most will be generalizations, as I do not wish to detail all the specifics because many of the churches, organizations (national or local), and volunteers have yet to be contacted and contracted. It would seem foolish for me to mention their names. Nonetheless, there is a plan in mind to take TWP from a local to regional level; then to a national level; and, I believe, an international level.

In addition to online resources in various forms, we are focused on three major groups.

First, our subscriber base which is the widowed community. We want to attract the widowed with free membership to the website and a free electronic subscription to our e-magazine. My hope is that it will eventually (quickly) grow to a printed magazine so that we can provide copies to those widows who do not use a computer or have internet access, and prefer a printed hard copy.

A hard copy serves many purposes: I envision church offices, counselor offices, senior centers, hospices, hospitals, and businesses locally and nationally that support TWP, also having a subscription – so that visitors and clients could become aware of their nonprofit support. A magazine would also provide additional exposure for advertising our national businesses and business owners. A magazine would help to brand us in the community, to churches, to the widowed and the nonprofit community. A magazine would also be an effective way to give recognition to our staff, board, and regional ambassadors. It will be a way of reaching out to the widowed community and into their homes.

Second, we want to partner with the Church and community organizations. We want to provide our resources to widows both directly and indirectly; and churches and organizations are the local representatives in their communities throughout the nation. Both churches and organizations will be the extension, the arms to the widowed in their community. Who better to connect with the widowed community than those who live among the widowed?

We also want to take a proactive approach to help local churches and community organizations find and attract the widowed. We are building relationships to help us accomplish this task locally. On our website will be a directory of all churches that have subscribed to TWP's resources and are providing our support group based curriculum to the widowed.

Third, we will perpetually partner with the business community—both local and national — to provide widows with ethical service and services. We believe that we have an obligation to our clients to provide them with the best service and services from a large spectrum of business categories. We especially hope to attract businesses from the faith community that understand our passion to care for the widowed Biblically.

Again, this will be a directory listing on our website, similar to an Angie's List or entities that have a preferred provider network. Each business will need to sign off by agreement to treat our clients "ethically, honestly", and hopefully provide a discount along with their services.

To assist churches and local organizations in establishing an extension of TWP, we will strive to provide and train a regional TWP ambassador. An ambassador's primary responsibilities will be threefold: 1.) build relationships with local churches and organizations; 2.) network with local businesses and business owners enlisting their support of TWP; and 3:) enroll local widows to membership with TWP.

Ambassadors will be trained via a web based video series that familiarizes them with the TWP organizational vision, the requirements of volunteering with TWP, as well as standards and expectations in representing us. Additionally, an ambassador might host TWP board members, advisory members, and selected professional guests at a Saturday conference to help launch TWP in several churches in a region. An ambassador would assist our executive staff in making the necessary accommodations for a weekend conference by making recommendations for a facility, hotel, and transportation.

We also want hope, inspiration, and resources to permeate our website, e-magazine, and online store. Such items as a monthly or daily calendar with inspirational Scripture and pictures, recommended books on issues related to widowhood, or condolence cards also help widows and their loved ones while branding TWP.

I can also imagine that some churches will want to customize the various avenues that they provide the widows of their community. For instance, a church may have an active youth group that wants to do service projects that could include things like doing a progressive car wash for all widows, or an adult group that wants to honor widows with a luncheon, or a benefactor that provides a turkey or ham to every widow at Thanksgiving, or a stamping club that makes cards to encourage and inspire widows, letting them know they are not alone. I am hoping to hear these kinds of stories from churches that add to the resources that we provide and personalize the service!

There is Biblical evidence and support regarding the importance of the Church to care for those who have suffered loss and are disadvantaged. Additionally, we should not only provide for them, but also protect them from those who would prey on and take advantage of them. I believe that we will see other residual benefits from serving widows.

The first dispute that the early church faced (and I don't consider the blending of Hebrew and Gentile into the Church, and the subsequent issue of circumcision to be the first internal dispute) was a cry of "favoritism" from the Hellenistic (Greek) Jews toward the native Hebrews.

I want TWP to partner with and be embraced by all denominations and cultures. I am hopeful that TWP will be diversified and fully blended racially. It would bring great joy to see all cultures and races represented in serving their widows with the love of Jesus. Our organization and its resources are available to everyone.

Can you imagine the Church arising and caring for the widowed like Jesus wants? We are honored to increase the awareness of the issue of widowhood and partner with churches and businesses all over the United States to uniquely serve widows with the love of Jesus.

We made history on February 25, 2017, when 30 friends (15 widowed and 15 pastors) attended a luncheon as our first event. It is my hope that you will catch our vision and partner with us as we build The Widows Project online community and safe places across our nation for your local widows to process widowhood. Together we can accomplish this vision!

Rolland Wright, President
The Widows Project
Rolland@thewidowsproject.org

CHAPTER 2

MEN WHO INFLUENCED
MY LIFE

Most would probably call me flippant if I were to say God led me to the founding of The Widows Project. I don't say that casually even though I feel it is a true statement. He did it through a combination of my own personal study of the Word, through authors of books that I have read and through what I have come to call Serendipity, planned appointments and Providence, timely preparation for future eventualities.

I'd like to explain and expand on the statement that I just made by saying that I deeply believe in God's foreknowledge and His personal involvement in our lives. I take great confidence in the declaration (prophecy) of Jeremiah (29:11) to the exiles (His covenant people) that had been taken to Babylon by Nebuchadnezzar when he said (under the inspiration of the Holy Spirit), "For I know the plans that I have for you...plans for welfare and not for calamity to give you a future and a hope." You might say, that promise was not meant for you. My response is that once I have been grafted in to the "cultivated olive tree" (Ro. 11:24) the promises given to His chosen people apply to me.

Over the past twelve years, I have been on a personal journey in establishing a lifestyle of daily reading the Bible and journaling that I discovered through a book by Wayne Cordeiro called, The Divine Mentor: Growing Your Faith as You Sit at the Feet of the Savior. I don't believe that the system he has developed is anything extraordinary.

In fact, it is quite simple in design but difficult in principle. Few will do it and master it. It is the art of daily submitting to the mirror of the Word. It is daily allowing the Holy Spirit to mentor you. It is submitting to the Lordship of Jesus. It is discipleship at the very core of our life. To those who are not truly born again, it is drudgery and foolishness. Even as a believer, when I was younger, I thought those who heralded the benefits of a daily time in the Word as legalists.

Now I rise early to protect that time and do so anxiously, eager to discover something new from the Word of God. Now I truly dine and feast at His table set before me.

I realize that before, I was starving myself and living in my own power. Now one of my favorite Scriptures is Acts 17:28, "For in Him we live and move and exist," or my paraphrase, have our very being. That is why I love the song written by Marie Barnett and popularized by Michael W. Smith, "Breathe."

In this rendition, Michael W. Smith asks: *"How many of you are hungry for God?"*

https://youtu.be/k8PBakPWph4

In another rendition, he says, *"I want more of Him. Who wants the flood gates to open up?"*

One of the "Beatitudes" is "Blessed are those who hunger and thirst for righteousness, for they shall be satisfied." One of the characteristics of a life that is longing for God is being hungry and thirst for Him. Pastor Cordeiro says in his book, "Eat fresh bread," when reading the Word of God (Cordeiro, 2008, p. 125).

Trust me; when you spend time in the Word of God, you cannot help but be changed—what Paul calls "transformation" (Rom. 12:1-2). I was taught many good, strong doctrinal truths about God, the Church, sin, and salvation; but was everything that I was taught the truth? What the application of Pastor Cordeiro's system has taught me is to think like a Berean (Acts 17:11). (I find it interesting that this verse is found in the same chapter as my favorite verse!) The Bereans had a lifestyle of "eagerness, examining the Scriptures daily, to see whether these things (what the Apostles were teaching) were so" (Acts 17:11). I believe that many church members, congregants and followers of a specific leader, would not believe what they think they believe if they also had a Berean lifestyle of "daily examining the Scriptures."

So, I credit Wayne Cordeiro for giving me some tools and explaining the why in his book for helping me establish a Berean lifestyle of daily examining the Scriptures from the Holy Bible.

It is from this lifestyle change that I came to see what I had been taught was not the "full gospel" but a partial gospel. What I mean by that is that I was taught that the imperative of the Gospel is the Great Commission found in Matthew 28: 18-20, that evangelism was king, end of story. Even then I understood the battle within the kingdom of God, the battle between those preaching evangelism as superior to those who claimed a social gospel and vice versa. What I have come to discover is that both sides became pharisaical.

Then another impactful author whom I hope to meet someday, and now fellow leader of an international nonprofit called World Vision, entered my life. Richard Stearns (2009) masterfully shares the necessity of the Church to care for the disadvantaged, the poor, the orphan, and the widow in his book, The Hole in Our Gospel: What Does God Expect of Us?

I remember as a youth hearing someone pray a prayer that went something like this: "Lord forgive our sins of commission (okay, I'm with you, these are the things that we have overtly done), and forgive our sins of omission (what is that?)." Well, I didn't investigate.

I know that I had heard the parable of the Good Samaritan, but somehow the parable was easy to ignore. The sin of the priest and the Levite was that they did nothing. Doing nothing is the great omission. Doing nothing was no longer an option for me.

So, with the awareness of Scripture and my responsibility for the disadvantaged, the really poor, the orphan and the widow, I struck out to see if I could find something that the Church, the community of faith, was not taking responsibility for—perhaps was walking right by and not noticing, and doing nothing or very little. I knew James 1:27, "This is pure and undefiled religion in the sight of God and Father, to visit orphans and widows in their distress, and to keep oneself unstained by the world."

I see advertising on late night television for the really poor third world children and orphans. There certainly is a real need, and I think that the pictures create a compelling, strongly emotional pull on everyone and rightfully so. But the word "widow" continued to stand out to me. What were we doing for the widowed? I saw organizations for specific widow groups like military personnel's widows, firefighters' widows, police officers' widows, and even deep sea fishermen's widows. But how about the rest of the widowed?

Another man I would like to meet someday is R.T. Kendall. I have read and consumed several of his books. I remember that it was his book, Total Forgiveness (Kendall, 2001), that I read first. It was very timely because I had just suffered the loss of two relationships almost simultaneously. Both were deeply impactful. I thought at that point in my life that I had the subject of forgiveness nailed, but I discovered that in both relationships I felt highly betrayed, and forgiveness did not come easily. Forgiveness is an extremely important issue in the life of all followers of Jesus. If you are one that has held a grudge for years, I encourage you to read this book; understand the power and freeing nature of forgiving.

We really don't have a choice if you read Matthew 6:9-15. Most of us know the Lord's Prayer, and many pastors ask us to recite it, and we do. But there are two verses following the Lord's Prayer that are vitally important! There is no other way to interpret them than to say, "If you forgive, you will be forgiven. But, if you do not forgive men, then your Father will not forgive your transgressions (sins)." This is non-negotiable with God. I think what attracts me to Dr. Kendall is not only his simple writing style, but also his spiritual path to where he is currently. I could identify with him because we had similar denominational paths, and had come from those theological structures to a charismatic lifestyle. That is why I appreciated his insights in his book, Holy Fire: A Balanced, Biblical Look at the Holy Spirit's work in Our Lives. I understood both sides of the argument that he so capably articulated. I agree that it is a "balanced biblical look at the Holy Spirit's work in our lives" (Kendall, 2014, p. Cover).

There is a fourth man that I would like to mention and give credit for where I am today. He is a man that came into my life in the twilight of his pastoral career. I perceived him as a gentle man, soft-spoken, highly competent, and knowledgeable of the Scriptures. He was a veteran preacher. I don't know the entirety of his career or history. But I made a discovery about him while doing some research while founding The Widows Project (TWP). In researching organizations that TWP might want to network with and/or partner with, I was reviewing the website for Bible Study Fellowship (BSF).

I was amazed to find that BSF credited this pastor, Dr. Ernest Hastings, with helping the founder of BSF, Audrey Wetherell Johnson, write the articles of incorporation and serving as a pastoral advisor for years. I had the pleasure of working with Dr. Hastings while he supplied the pulpit for about six months for Queen Anne Baptist Church in Seattle. I felt like this was the purpose for our paths crossing. Even though it was only for a short period of time that we interacted, it felt to me that it was not a chance meeting but rather a purposed meeting. Dr. Hastings is deceased, but I felt like there was a passing of heritage by association with him.

I mentioned at the beginning of this chapter that serendipity and providence have surrounded my life, and these are four distinct men that have touched my life. One I have met, the others I only know from the pages of their books. But each has had his distinct impact on my life, orchestrated by a very personal God.

An additional evidence of God's serendipity and providence of an ever-abiding confidence and peace that founding The Widows Project is purposed – is the number of people that continue to "appear" as a help or resource to build the foundation or what we call infrastructure today. There are too many to mention, and my concern is leaving someone out. Suffice to say, that each of them as they appear make me smile and confirm within the words of that still, small voice that has told me, "You have everything that you need; and if you build it, they will come."

I say a heartfelt thank you to all who have chosen to participate in the formation of TWP. You are a serendipitous and a providentially provided servant! To those whom I have known as widowed in all the years previous, I want to ask your forgiveness for not seeing you, not acknowledging your loss, not having compassion, not founding The Widows Project sooner.

CHAPTER 3

WIDOWS OF THE BIBLE

Widows tend to be transparent or nearly invisible. And unless one is paying specific attention to noticing widows in Scripture, you can almost miss them. Allow me to draw attention to the nearly invisible.

The various terms associated with a widow appear approximately 90 times: widow 59 times; widowed once; widowhood twice; widow's 30 times, and widows' thrice. Never did I find the term widower in Scripture. There certainly would be widowers in the Old Testament, as we evidence Lot's wife looking back to Sodom and Gomorrah when she had been instructed not to look, and was subsequently turned into a pillar of salt (Gen. 19: 26). Sarah preceded Abraham in death (Gen. 23: 1-2). Rachel preceded Israel (Gen. 35: 16-20). The nameless wife of Samson preceded him (Judges 15: 6). Finally, Michal preceded David (2 Sam. 6:23). I think we would have to ascertain that in the Hebrew culture the wife relied on her husband for life, protection, and wellbeing.

I find it interesting that the initial problem the early Church had to resolve (post ascension) was a dispute between the "Hellenistic Jews against the native Hebrews, because their widows were being overlooked in the daily serving of food" (Acts 6:1-7). It was from this dispute that the 12, Apostles, with wisdom, did not get distracted from "the word of God in order to serve tables," but delegated to the congregation the responsibility to select seven men "full of faith and of the Holy Spirit." This account is our introduction to Stephen and Philip but not the last that we hear from them.

I mentioned earlier that widows are almost invisible unless one is paying attention. In my studying widows in Scripture, I found one such widow in the Gospels. She has a very prominent but kind of obscure setting at the dedication of Jesus. She gets to observe from a vantage point that few would get to see Jesus.

Let me set the stage. Jesus is eight days old, and Mary and Joseph are taking the Christ child to Jerusalem to the temple to be circumcised and dedicated to "the Lord," and to offer sacrifice according to the Law of the Lord, "A pair of turtledoves, or two young pigeons." And beginning in vs. 25 of Luke 2: (NASB)

25 And behold, there was a man in Jerusalem whose name was Simeon; and this man was righteous and devout, looking for the consolation of Israel; and the Holy Spirit was upon him.

26 And it had been revealed to him by the Holy Spirit that he would not see death before he had seen the Lord's Christ.

27 And he came in the Spirit into the temple; and when the parents brought in the child Jesus, to carry out for Him the custom of the law,

28 then he took Him into his arms, and blessed God, and said,

29 now, Lord, thou dost let thy bondservant depart in peace, according to Thy word;

30 for my eyes have seen Thy salvation,

31 which thou hast prepared in the presence of all peoples,

32 a light of revelation to the Gentiles, and the glory of thy people Israel.

33 And his father and mother were amazed at the things which were being said about him.

34 And Simeon blessed them, and said to Mary his mother, behold, this child is appointed for the fall and rise of many in Israel, and for a sign to be opposed,

35 (and a sword will pierce even your own soul) to the end that thoughts from many hearts may be revealed.

Anna

Most of us have stopped right there at the end of verse 35 and not benefitted from the whole story. For in the next three obscure verses we are told about a widow that was blessed with the best viewing point in the temple. This is like getting a 50-yard line, box seat tickets for the Seahawks, or seats behind the plate at Dodger stadium, or midcourt seats to see LeBron James. The widow's name was Anna, and here is what we are told:

36 And there was a prophetess, Anna the daughter of Phanuel, of the tribe of Asher. She was advanced in years, having lived with a husband seven years after her marriage,

37 And then as a widow to the age of eighty-four. And she never left the temple, serving night and day with fastings and prayers.

38 And at that very moment she came up and began giving thanks to God, and continued to speak of Him to all those who were looking for the redemption of Jerusalem. (NASB)

Can you imagine all those years of service, culminating into seeing?! And while the text is silent, can you really believe that she didn't hold Jesus? God incarnate, the "consolation of Israel?" Here we see a widow filled with praise, "giving thanks to God," and she couldn't stop speaking of Him "to all who were looking for the redemption of Jerusalem."

Hallelujah! You know how a baby can light up a room! Now, multiply that by a factor of 10 and we are getting close. Jesus was more than a baby…He was God in the flesh!

Had you paid attention to Anna before today? If not, I hope you took notice that she was standing there observing the whole dedication, and then she joined in the celebration "giving thanks to God." I hope that you can celebrate with her!

Ruth

Probably the most prominent widow in all of the Bible is Ruth. If you are not aware, Ruth is the great grandmother of David. According to Matthew 1:1-17, we can establish that Ruth was the great- (times 29) grandmother of Jesus. Verse 17 establishes that *"from Abraham to David are fourteen generations; and from David to the deportation to Babylon fourteen generations; and from the deportation to Babylon to the time of Christ fourteen generations."* (NASB)

There are a number of facets to the story of Ruth that are fascinating; and I have to admit that, while I knew Ruth was a great-grandmother to David and her relationship to Jesus, I hadn't really paid attention to her. Again, I think we are historically guilty of ignoring widows, even those who are prominent and important in the lineage of Jesus. If Ruth did not meet Boaz; and Boaz did not redeem Ruth, and together would not have produced a male child, then the lineage would likely have been is broken.

Just as Ruth is faithful to her mother- in-law Naomi, so is God faithful to His covenant to David. It is not just coincidental that as the story of Ruth unfolds, we are told that Naomi has a husband named Elimelech, and that they have two sons – Mahlon and Chilion – who marry Moabite women as they travel through the land of Moab. The names of their wives were Ruth and Orpah. We are told that Elimelech dies, and the sons both live ten years after being married, and then they die. All three women are widowed. Naomi decides to return to Judah and encourages her two daughters-in-law to stay, find husbands, and remarry. Orpah elects to stay but Ruth is famously quoted as saying:

"Do not urge me to leave you or turn back from following you; for where you go, I will go, and where you lodge, I will lodge. Your people shall be my people, and your God, my God. Where you die, I will die, and there I will be buried. Thus, may the Lord do to me, and worse, if anything but death parts you and me." Ruth 1:16-17

So, they journey to Bethlehem. Isn't that a coincidence! Where was it prophesied that Jesus would be born? Bethlehem. Another coincidence: Bethlehem is translated "house of bread." Isn't it interesting that the "Bread of Life" should be born in the house of bread?

The providence of God flows through the lives of Ruth, Naomi, and Boaz. Another coincidence is that Boaz just happens to be a wealthy relative of Naomi's now deceased husband. Boaz is interested in Ruth because he sees in her "a woman of excellence" (Ruth 3:11).

There is one glitch. There is one relative that is in line ahead of Boaz and he must approach him and offer him the opportunity to buy Naomi's property – a field – and along with that property "acquire Ruth the Moabitess, the widow of the deceased, in order to raise up the name of the deceased on his inheritance. And the closest relative said, *"I cannot redeem it for myself, lest I jeopardize my own inheritance. Redeem it for yourself; you may have my right of redemption, for I cannot redeem it."* Ruth 4:5-6

Boaz redeems Ruth and the land, marries her, and together they produce a male heir that continues the lineage to David! This birth is just as important as the birth of David. For without Obed, we wouldn't have Jesse, and then we wouldn't have David. This is the pure, providential nature of God! Oh, and one other observation: For those of us who are Gentile believers and believe that it wasn't until the New Testament that God grafted us in or included us in His Salvation plan, remember that Ruth was a Moabitess.

Who were the Moabites? According to the Holman Bible Dictionary (Brand, Draper, & England, 2003), "Moabites were despised by the Israelites because of their incestuous origin" (Gen. 1:30-38), "their hostility to the Israelites when they came out of Egypt" (Num. 22-24; Deut. 23: 3-6), and "their seduction of the Israelites into physical and spiritual adultery" (Num. 25: 1-9). And yet God included a Gentile blood in His lineage. *"Through Boaz and Ruth not only was a threatened family rescued from extinction, but through them God prepared the way for David, and ultimately David's greatest son, Jesus the Messiah"* (Brand, Draper, & England, 2003, p. 1424).

The Widow & Elijah

I'd like to highlight another widow found in the Old Testament. This widow lived in the Mediterranean seacoast town of Zerephath, just south of Sidon. The name of the town possibly meant, "smelting, or refining." It was to this town that Elijah fled at God's command after prophesying a drought in 1 Kings 17:1, that continued "severely" for three years according to 1 Kings 18:2.

This drought came upon Israel due to the actions of the seventh king of Israel's Northern Kingdom, Ahab, of which 1 Kings 17:30 says, he "did evil in the sight of the Lord more than all who were before him." You see, he first of all married a Phoenician princess named Jezebel. Her father Ethbaal was the king of Sidon. And when she married Ahab, she not only removed any military threat from Phoenicia, but also brought her pagan deities with her, as evidenced by Ahab building her a temple for Baal.

This was a complete spiritual compromise on Ahab's part. Her name, because of her character, has come to be associated with wickedness because she is credited with the massacre of the Lord's prophets (1 Kings 18:4, 19), and the seizure of an Israelite's land (1 Kings 21).

So, it was because of the drought that Elijah was told by God in 1 Kings 17:9-16, "*Arise, go to Zarephath, which belongs to Sidon, and stay there; behold, I have commanded a widow there to provide for you.*" I hope you see some irony in that Scripture. God had "commanded" a widow there to provide for Elijah. Someone who had very limited resources.

Elijah had just come from hiding himself at God's direction, in the area of the "brook Cherith, which is east of Jordan." There he would have water and providential provision from "ravens." God had commanded the ravens to feed Elijah. And it says, "The ravens brought him bread and meat in the morning and bread and meat in the evening, and he would drink from the brook." This sustained Elijah until the drought caused the brook to dry up.

So now, God sends Elijah to a second unlikely source to be provided for, because we are told that as Elijah got to the "gate of the city, behold, a widow (we never are told her name), was there gathering sticks, and he called to her and said, please get me a little water in a jar, that I may drink, (and oh, while you are at it), and please bring me a piece of bread in your hand."

Her response is priceless, "*But she said, 'As the Lord your God lives, I have no bread, only a handful of flour in the bowl and a little oil in the jar, and behold, I am gathering a few sticks that I may go in and prepare for me and my son, that we may eat it and die.'*" Did you catch that last part…"that we may eat it and die"? This widow was hopeless and expecting to die. Here she was, preparing what she was anticipating to be her and her son's last meal, and this prophet of God was asking her to feed him. I have to believe that while God told Elijah that the widow was going to provide for him, God knew the truth of the woman's condition.

If you are a widow or widower, and you are reading this and feeling just as hopeless as this widow, I want you to take notice of how God, thru Elijah, supernaturally provides for her, her son, and Elijah. After the widow tells Elijah in complete transparency that she is fixing their last meal to eat it and die, Elijah tells her, "Do not fear; go, do as you have said, but make me a little bread cake from it first, and bring it out to me, and afterward you may make one for yourself and for your son."

Don't you think that she was thinking, "Elijah, you must not have heard me, I only have enough for my son and myself." Elijah probably repeated to her, "Do not fear." "*For thus says the Lord God of Israel, the bowl of flour shall not be exhausted, nor shall the jar of oil be empty, until the day that the Lord sends rain on the face of the earth. So, she went* (and exercised faith in doing as the prophet had told her) *and did according to the word of Elijah, and she and he and her household ate for many days.*"

In faith, she did what Elijah prophesied to her, and "she, and he (Elijah) and her household (her son) ate for many days." They were sustained supernaturally. No one died. The text doesn't even say that they heard their stomachs growl. The last verse sums it up, *"The bowl of flour was not exhausted* (it did not deplete)*, nor did the jar of oil become empty, according to the word of the Lord which He* (God) *spoke through Elijah"*.

You may stand in need of a miracle because of what you may feel is hopeless. I want to believe with you and for you that God stands ready to meet your needs just like the widow of Zarephath. It is my hope that God will meet needs like this through The Widows Project, the area churches, and community organizations that we partner with.

You may have heard of a radio program years ago by Paul Harvey called "The Rest of The Story." I started to wrap up the account of the widow from Zarephath and realized that I had closed shop a bit early. Closing early on a verse of Scripture is one of my pet peeves with preachers in particular. We like to make our point instead of letting the full passage represent itself in full.

This nameless widow had a nameless son, and during the time that Elijah was with them, her son became "severely sick; so sick that there was no breath left in him." Here is how the "rest of the story" unfolds (1 Kings 17: 18-24)

18 So she said to Elijah, what do I have to do with you, O man of God? You have come to me to bring my iniquity to remembrance and to put my son to death!"

19 He said to her, give me your son. Then he took him from her bosom and carried him up to the upper room where he was living, and laid him on his own bed.

20 He called to the Lord and said, O Lord my God, have you also brought calamity to the widow with whom I am staying, by causing her son to die?

21 Then he stretched himself upon the child three times, and called to the Lord and said, O Lord my God, I pray you, let this child's life return to him.

22 The Lord heard the voice of Elijah, and the life of the child returned to him, and he revived.

23 Elijah took the child and brought him down from the upper room into the house and gave him to his mother; and Elijah said, see, your son is alive.

24 Then the woman said to Elijah, now I know that you are a man of God, and that the word of the Lord in your mouth is truth. (NASB)

God not only sustained her and her son's life with supernatural provision, He raised her son from death thru Elijah, and he presented her son "alive." It wasn't a conventional method that Elijah used. In fact, in our era, "stretching" oneself upon a child three times would not be seen as p.c. Nor would calling upon the Lord praying, "Let this child's life return." Twice now, God has presented Himself supernaturally to the widow and her son.

God has many names in Hebrew. He has many names because His nature and character are so vast. The following examples are a sampling of God's names that are found in the Old Testament (secured from the Blue Letter Bible):

El Shaddai (Lord God Almighty)
El Elyon (The Most High God)
Adonai (Lord, Master)
Yahweh (Lord, Jehovah)
Jehovah Nissi (The Lord My Banner)
Jehovah-Raah (The Lord My Shepherd)
Jehovah Rapha (The Lord That Heals)
Jehovah Shammah (The Lord Is There)
Jehovah Tsidkenu (The Lord Our Righteousness)
Jehovah Mekoddishkem (The Lord Who Sanctifies You)
El Olam (The Everlasting God)
Elohim (God)
Qanna (Jealous)
Jehovah Jireh (The Lord Will Provide)
Jehovah Shalom (The Lord Is Peace)
Jehovah Sabaoth (The Lord of Hosts)

Certainly, from the widow's perspective, she witnessed fully the "provision and the healing" nature of the Lord. Her final words are captured as saying to Elijah, "Now I know that you are a man of God, and that the word of the Lord in your mouth is truth."

Tabitha (Dorcas)

A supreme example of the "reputation for good works" is found in Acts 9: 32-42. Peter is traveling throughout the surrounding area of Lydda and in the power of the Holy Spirit, Peter facilitates the physical healing of a man name Aeneas. "All who lived in Lydda and Sharon witnessed this miracle healing and "they turned to the Lord." At this same time a woman known as Tabitha – an Aramaic name meaning "gazelle", translated in Greek is called Dorcas – "fell sick and died." This woman was known for "abounding with deeds of kindness and charity", which she continually did.

Though the text does not tell us if she is a widow, several Bible references such as Easton's Bible Dictionary refer to her as a pious widow.

The text gives us some insight into what Tabitha did. She was a seamstress, and was known for the "tunics and garments" that she made while she was with them.

She reminds me of a lady that I knew in a church years ago. She made infant blankets for all the mothers as a gift for the birth of their baby. She literally made hundreds of these blankets with her knitting needles. She, like Tabitha, had a reputation. Tabitha's death caused a great amount of grief among the widows in that area. I can only assume their grief was fueled by her "acts of good works." She had touched their lives.

Peter sent all the grieving widows out of the room, and again in the power of the Spirit says, "'Tabitha arise.' And she opened her eyes, and when she saw Peter, she sat up." The Lord restored Tabitha to her friends.

The whole issue of a good reputation is paramount to be included on this leadership list. Tabitha embodied the model of a woman whose reputation was built upon good works.

Mary

What a critical position Mary plays in the earthly life of Jesus. Of all people that were touched by Jesus while on earth, Mary knew who Jesus was. Only one woman in the history of mankind was privileged to be appointed as the one through whom Christ was born. Her response recorded in Luke 1:38 says much about her character, "Behold, the bond-slave of the Lord; be it done to me according to your word." (NASB)

In response to being told that she would be the Lord's instrument, she travels to see her cousin, Elizabeth, who was also pregnant with a long-awaited child. As they greeted one another, the Bible says regarding Elizabeth's child, "...the baby (John) leaped in her womb; and Elizabeth was filled with the Holy Spirit" (Luke 1:41). And prophetically (I believe) Elizabeth shouted, "Blessed among women are you and blessed is the fruit of your womb!" (Luke 1:42).

It seems that in the spirit Elizabeth said this not knowing that Mary was pregnant; for her question following the statement is one of inquiry, "And how has it happened to me, that the mother of my Lord should come to me?" (Luke 1:43). Elizabeth asks no more questions and immediately chimes into more prophetic utterance, "For behold, when the sound of your greeting reached my ears, the baby leaped in my womb for joy. And blessed is she who believes that there would be a fulfillment of what been spoken to her by the Lord."

The prophetic nature of Elizabeth's words launches Mary into a prophetic response unlike any recorded response in Scriptures. Listen and rejoice with Mary as Luke shares her praise:

46 And Mary said: "My soul exalts the Lord,

47 And my spirit has rejoiced in God my Savior.

48 "For He has had regard for the humble state of His bondslave;

For behold, from this time on all generations will count me blessed.

49 "For the Mighty One has done great things for me;

And holy is His name.

50 "And His mercy is upon generation after generation

Toward those who fear Him.

51 "He has done mighty deeds with His arm;

He has scattered those who were proud in the thoughts of their heart.

52 "He has brought down rulers from their thrones,

And has exalted those who were humble.

53 "He has filled the hungry with good things;

And sent away the rich empty-handed.

54 "He has given help to Israel His servant,

In remembrance of His mercy,

55 As He spoke to our fathers,

To Abraham and his descendants forever." (Luke 1:46-55 NASB)

"For He has regarded the humble state of his bond-slave." What powerful words from a young woman. We do not see a single ounce of fear or anxiety or hesitation over what has happened in her life. In an instant, her life has been changed forever, and forever she will be blessed.

Not only was Mary the mother of Jesus, but also at His crucifixion, we know that Mary stood at the foot of the cross as a widow. Historians believe Joseph probably died prior to Jesus' public ministry, as we see no mention of him at key points in Scripture where Mary is mentioned – like the wedding in John 2 or Jesus' crucifixion in John 19:25-27.

As we observe Jesus on the cross, there are only seven sayings that Jesus made, and two were directed to specific people. One statement to one of the convicts and one to "the disciple" (unnamed, but we know that was a characteristic of John's writing). Jesus said, "Woman (directed to Mary), behold your son (directed to John)! Then He said to the disciple, behold your mother! And from that hour the disciple took her into his own household."

What was Jesus telling us and telling John? I believe that Jesus was demonstrating to us Exodus 20:12, the fifth commandment, "Honor your father and mother." Jesus told us, "Do not think that I came to abolish the law or the prophets, I did not come to abolish but to fulfill (Matt. 5:17). He passed to John the care of His mother. He did not leave her alone without provision.

I have wondered why we did not see James at the foot of the cross and Jesus passing the care of His mother to James. Could it be that Jesus' brothers were not believers at the time of his crucifixion? Or, was Jesus foreshadowing a distinction between our biological family and a new spiritual family? If so, that explains why He would not commit the care of Mary to one of his brothers. I believe it is because Jesus had heralded the new covenant and new life. Mary's care was entrusted to those who Jesus knew were included into the new kingdom.

However, we see recorded in I Cor. 15:7 Jesus's appearance to James, his half-brother. Did that meeting make a difference? Well, James went on to write the book named after him and contains a frequently quoted verse in James 1:27, "This is pure and undefiled religion in the sight of our God and Father, to visit the orphans and widows in their distress, and to keep oneself unstained by the world." To hear the transition of James' life to a deeper level of resolve, one only needs to read the first verse of his book, "James, a bond-servant of God and of the Lord Jesus Christ." James also went on to die a martyr's death.

Mary holds a prominent place in Scripture, not only as the mother of Jesus, but also as a widow.

CHAPTER 4

WIDOWS WHO IMPACTED MY LIFE

"Grannie" Annie T.

In preparing to write this chapter, I took some time to reflect over my life to see whether there were widows that had influenced or impacted my childhood or youth.

Almost instantly, my thoughts led me to fondly remember a woman that worked with the youth ministry of the church I grew up in. She was affectionately called "Granny Annie" because she adopted all of us and treated us as if we were her grandchildren. I don't know her story and never met her husband, but I know that she deeply cared for all of us. She was not greeted as a pastor nor given the title, but she counseled us, organized activities, taught us from the Bible, and ferried us by car everywhere. Most of all, she gave everyone attention and love.

You would never forget Granny Annie if you met her. She was a unique personality, and I think that she needed us as much as we needed her. Allow me to paint a picture for you of who Granny Annie was.

If you are a baby boomer, then you probably watched the television programs Hee Haw or the Grand Ole Opry. You will recall a personality by the name of Minnie Pearl. Minnie was known for her loud, high pitched voice, her greeting to her audience, "Howdy, I'm so please to be here!", her dress style, and her hat that still had the price tag dangling from the front and side.

Today we would call it her "brand." Minnie Pearl was one of a kind, and so was Granny Annie. In fact, Granny Annie would many times entertain us with her imitation of Minnie Pearl. You couldn't help but smile and laugh.

Patricia (Pat) Brown

There are few people that have had a bigger impact on my life than Pat Brown. Relationships like the one I had with her don't just happen. I believe in serendipity, which I define as God-planned appointments. Pat was one of those "God-planned" meetings. I don't recall exactly when or how this all came about, but I know why we met. Pat was a member of Queen Anne Baptist Church in Seattle where I was an associate pastor in the late '90s. I had just gone through a divorce, at which time Pat and I adopted and befriended each other. I say it that way because she was the age of my parents, and I treated her like a mother.

I didn't know at the time, but later discovered that she had lost a son that I had never met. While she had two biological children who were both married and had children, and lived in the greater Seattle area, my parents also lived about an hour away. We had a special bond that didn't replace our biological families but met a need in both of us.

I also believe in the providence of God, and I define that as God's ability to see the beginning to the end and, knowing the big picture, has preordained and foreordained our lives. I'll never forget the day when I was working for a local painting contractor, and we finished a job early. I recall being prompted to stop by Pat's home, and upon arriving discovered she wasn't home. I rang her doorbell and was returning to my vehicle when she returned home. She got out of her little maroon car and started crying. She had just been to her doctor, who told her that she had ovarian cancer.

No one will ever be able to convince me differently that our encounter that day wasn't God-ordained. We cried together, and I tried to comfort and console her. It was a dark time in her life, and I wish that I knew then what I know now. I treated her as a second mother and brought her hanging baskets for Mother's Day to hang around her patio. She included me as another son, inviting me to many family events.

I believe that Pat had the gift of "hospitality." On many Friday or Saturday evenings, she hosted people who didn't have family, or were friends from her years of administrative work in the public school district in Seattle. She had quite a circle of friends and kept an active life. She made everyone feel at home and part of an extended family — all of this on top of her own biological kids and grandkids.

Pat was a gamer. Most of those Friday or Saturday evenings, not only did we share a meal, but also the evening was capped with Mexican Train Dominoes. I have always loved board games and those evenings reminded me of my own childhood when my family would play games, especially over the holidays. Games like ping pong, Chinese checkers, Rook, Karom, Uno, and Yahtzee.

I will always remember her for the seafood that I was blessed to share with her. Her son Steve is a fisherman and learned it from his dad. Pat was the beneficiary of much salmon and Dungeness crabs, because Steve parked his boat at her home. Barbecues were a frequent experience during the summer on her patio!

While I remember the social gatherings, the food and games, it was Pat's friendship and love that touched me most. We shared many a conversation about life and spiritual things. She taught me that we have room and enough love to have additional sons and mothers. There are people all around us that are lonely or hurting and need the additional comfort and friendship. I find that many widows are separated from their family by distance or relationally disenfranchised from their children. I am grateful to Pat's children that they shared their mom with me.

Margaret N.

I knew Margaret and her husband Ralph, in the mid-1990s. They also attended a Queen Anne Baptist Church where I was ministering during that time. I know Ralph's career was as a concrete contractor, and that he worked on the Kingdome, Seattle's domed stadium that was demolished in 2000 and replaced by the current Seahawk Stadium. After Ralph's passing, Margaret and I kept in touch, and on several occasions had conversations on spiritual things. One topic that several of these conversations centered on was dreams and what significance they have in our lives.

Margaret told me of life in the Canadian plains above the Dakotas and later life in Spokane, Washington. She related a dream that she had then as a younger woman. I don't recall the details, but I enjoyed the conversation. We shared other times, meals and social events like the Christmas bell choir concert we attended together.

Marilyn H.

Music has been a constant theme throughout my life. In 1995, I began a five year music ministry relationship with a Baptist church in Seattle. Marilyn had been the organist at this church ever since she was a young woman. She had been married to a fisherman whom I never met. Marilyn was a unique combination of church musician, music teacher and animal lover. As a Church Musician, she had faithfully served the Church for over 50 years. She also taught youth piano lessons and had done so for many years.

As an animal lover, Marilyn had a small farm about 40 miles north of Seattle. On this farm she had cattle, cats, a dog named Minnie that accompanied her to church on Sundays and Wednesdays at rehearsals, and Arabian horses. The pride of her stable was a miniature stallion by the name of Mr. Stubbs. I never did meet Mr. Stubbs but I did see his pictures. As you can imagine, I was told that he thought he was as big as any full-sized stallion. Her animals were members of her family, and she loved them all intensely.

The things I remember about Marilyn are her faithfulness and devotion to God, in her service to the Church and to others. She had a large circle of friends in the Church, from the years of teaching music lessons and in the horse world. She was always supportive of my leadership. I don't recall ever hearing a critical word from her. I am glad that God purposed our paths to meet.

Lois H.

I met Lois on my 10-week vacation to Portugal in the summer of 2015. Lois is British but has lived in Portugal for about 15 years. One could not meet Lois and forget her. She possesses a larger-than-life persona. She has a wealth of knowledge, she has a heart for the nation of Israel, and for those who minister to the kingdom of God.

She reminds me a bit of my paternal grandmother. Both possess great energy and resolve. Both are strong personalities. My grandmother earned a Master's degree in the 1950s, and in her later years was driving people younger than her to appointments.

Lois does the same and has greater energy than most her age. Lois is unique, as she has experienced widowhood twice, once before she came to Christ and once after. From the first time we met, she extended her hospitality. On my third visit, she opened her home to me. We shared many a morning conversation and breakfast on her balcony patio. I was introduced to the Cape gooseberry and had many of them on my cereal.

I felt as if her home was a combination sabbatical retreat and seminary library. I consumed a number of her books while staying in her home. It was a valuable time of learning. Lois isn't wealthy by worldly standards, but she is rich in friends, in church family, and in Christ.

"Charlie" Charles B.

I met Charlie in the early 1990s when he was already in his 90s. He was a member of a Baptist church that I was attending, and he took me into his home. We shared some good times together. Charlie loved the Lord. Every morning he would sit at his dining room table and read a daily entry from Oswald Chambers' (1935) "My Utmost for His Highest". If my schedule allowed me to join him for breakfast, he would many times read that day's offering. He would then sit back and comment on how much Oswald had waxed eloquent on that day's Scriptural topic.

Charlie was a sharp-witted man and used to poke fun at himself. One day, I remember him saying, "I still have all my marbles, but I think I've lost my taw." He frequently would sit at his piano and tickle the ivories. Sometimes he would play a hymn, but usually he would play music from his era. Charlie didn't talk about himself much, but he mentioned to me several times that he had a brother who played and directed bands in the Big Band Era. He also talked affectionately about his wife whom I never met.

Charlie was what I would call a sophisticated gentleman and a Texan. His hair was white and combed back. He sported a mustache and wire rim glasses, and he always wore a hat and walked with the aid of a cane. Every Wednesday, he went to lunch with our pastor, whom he acknowledged with the name Preston, the Canadian word for pastor. I learned sometime after his passing that Charlie was listed in the Who's Who of Southern Baptists for his work with Baptist men. Charlie touched my life at a time when I needed compassion. He was a serendipity – a planned appointment of God's.

Doris S.

Doris is one of those precious-in-God's-sight type of people. She had a huge heart for God and for missions. I knew Doris only in her later years, but you could always count on the fact that, when she saw you, she would light up, make a beeline toward you, and give you a big hug. She genuinely loved people and was a child at heart. She was greatly loved by her Church family, and it was sad to watch her decline as dementia took its toll.

I recall one evening that she arrived at church disoriented, and one of the men noticed that she had walked to church. He asked her where her car was, and she didn't know. He went looking for it and found it several blocks away — in gear, with the engine still running. Do I believe in guardian angels? Yes.

Janice K.

I knew Janice and Ellis (married couple), and they were always kind to me. Ellis loved whenever my parents visited Queen Anne Baptist Church (QABC) because they were both retirees of long careers with the Boeing Company. My dad and Ellis would exchange stories about their experiences of the "good ole" days of Boeing, and especially the 747 program.

The one unique thing about QABC was the number of couples that had 50-, 60-, and 70-year marriages. For a church their size, it was uncanny the number of long-term marriages. Janice was by nature a quiet, supportive wife and member of QABC. She sang in the choir that I directed, including the numerous Easter cantatas and Christmas musicals.

Most congregations of Baptist churches that I have been associated with like to eat! QABC was no exception. They had a weekly Wednesday evening meal that couples took turns hosting. In conjunction with that meal, once a year they had a talent and hobby show. Janice had a unique hobby. She liked to collect rolling pins. Her collection included glass, metal, and wood rolling pins for making noodles, cookies, and baked goods. I remember being in an antique shop in Arkansas and spotting a rolling pin used to make donuts. I immediately thought of Janice, purchased it, and sent it to her to add to her collection.

Ferol H.

I like people that have unique, unusual, one-of-a-kind names like mine. While I was at QABC, Ferol was married to her long-time mate,

Robert (Bob). Bob had one of those deep bass voices that would have been good on radio. Ferol and Bob several times used my contractor services to do some interior and exterior painting at their home on Queen Anne. They always invited me to share a meal with them and were most hospitable. They also introduced me to their neighbors who also had me do some painting for them.

I'll never forget a Christmas some years ago when they invited a group of QABC people over to see their production in the basement. I had heard about it, but it was another thing to actually see it. Bob had created a model train display with a complete town, and no detail was missing. It was quite a treat to see something that was so meticulously put together.

Florence H.

Florence is another widow that I knew as part of a married couple to Les. They, too, are one of the long-term married couples at QABC. They were a striking couple and loved to dance, and did so even well up into their 80s. Florence is a redhead, and I called her my favorite redhead (and she was Les' too). They always seemed to have a smile. Years before I knew Florence, I was told that she, for years, used to be a designer for the Bon Marche stores in Seattle. So, you can imagine what Christmas and Easter looked like at QABC. It easily was the best decorated church that I have ever been a part of. It was elegant, classy and represented her love for God and His Church.

Jim S.

I would be remiss if I did not include Jim in this list and chapter. Jim is a silver haired Hawaiian, a handsome man and as old-school as they come. He says what he means and means what he says. He is fiercely loyal and comes from an era of respect for the military, country, and God. He is proud of his family's military careers and his heritage. He is caring and protective of his friends and family. I have always felt deeply valued and respected by Jim. He has gone to bat for me several times, and has kept in touch with me over the years since leaving QABC. He has been an anchor at QABC for many years, and has always been hospitable to me and a friend. I want him to know that I value his friendship deeply.

Mamie R.

Mamie is my maternal grandmother. I didn't know Mamie well, and I didn't know her much as a widow. I think it is fair to say that both of my grandfathers died prematurely and lived tough lives as farmers in the Midwest. It was probably equally tough for my grandmothers too. I know that Mamie had six children – five girls, one boy – and that my mother was the eldest of the six.

I remember that my grandparents came to Washington twice, and that we attended the 1962 World's Fair in Seattle on one trip. We then spent a few days camping on the Washington coast on another trip.

On trips to their Nebraska farm, I remember things like milking cows and collecting eggs from the henhouse. I helped with everything that involved filling the freezer with hens (I'm being nice; and yes, I have seen a chicken running with its…well, you understand). I learned what an electric fence does when you touch it, or even a barbed wire fence for that matter. I learned to run a milk separator and slopped the hogs. I learned to bale hay and drive a tractor. I learned to ride their palomino. I learned that having a breakfast that was as big as any dinner included real cream on your cereal.

I remember after Grandma was widowed that she was traveling through Ellensburg, Washington. I was in college at Central Washington College (before it was a university), and I was sitting on a charter bus with the CWC choir getting ready to tour, when one of the students called out my name. They said my grandmother was there. I was stunned by her spontaneous presence, since I didn't know of her travels.

This was the last time I saw her alive. She looked good. In fact, she looked probably ten years younger than I had recalled her the last time I had seen her. We had just a brief few moments, as she just caught the bus just before we left on tour. Apparently, she had gone to my dorm first, and someone let her know that I was over at the Music Hall and about to go on tour. I'm glad she caught me, because it was the final time to see her.

Even though I feel I didn't know her well, I still felt something special for her. I knew that she was my grandmother. I had the privilege of singing at her funeral. In this rural town of Allen, Nebraska, we had the service in the church. We then walked right out back of the church and held the burial ceremony. This was the only time I have experienced that particular convenience.

Dora Yvonne Elaine W.

I think that anyone that needs multiple middle names to define themselves has to be a character, and Grandma Wright had a lot of character. Both of my grandmothers were strong personalities. Dora had four children, taught in a one-room schoolhouse early in her career, was raised by farmers, married a farmer, and well, knew it all. She was a self-proclaimed…well, she knew it all, and/or at least had an opinion to share.

I will say this: She was way ahead of her time. Here was a woman who had a Master's degree, which was unusual for a woman in the 1940s and 50s. She was married to a man that had perhaps a second grade education. She sold World Book encyclopedias during the summer. She was a juicer by 1960. I spent one summer at age 6 or 7 with my grandparents, and I remember having to drink a glass of carrot juice everyday straight; nothing cutting the taste. In her later years, she taught special education in the city of Lakefield, Minnesota.

That summer I spent with my grandparents was also filled with memories of doing daily chores: mostly weeding soybeans, playing at

Spirit Lake on their property, catching fireflies and night crawlers (bigger than any worms I've seen in Washington), and seeing the Black Angus cattle.

I also remember taking baths in a round, galvanized washtub in the kitchen. They didn't have running water or indoor plumbing, so, water was fetched from the well pump, and then the tea kettle was used to add some hot water. You always wanted to be the first one in the tub, because the water wasn't changed between bathers. It was a bathing experience.

She had more energy than 10 Scandinavian women half her size! Her maiden name was Gronlund, and she had a laugh that was a full-on laugh. She didn't cheat herself, and this ran in the family. I used to love watching my dad watch Looney Tunes cartoons. He would laugh so hard that tears would be flowing down his cheeks. Into her late 80s, Grandma Wright was driving the elderly to their doctor appointments. Her family has great genes, though. Her siblings have all lived into their 90s.

There was faith on both sides of my family, and for that I am grateful. I can recall that the summer I spent with my grandparents, they had a ritual every night. We always had a bowl of cereal and read a chapter out of the Bible, out-loud together, and then said a prayer before bed.

I'm grateful for my grandparents on both sides. Without them, my parents wouldn't exist; and that precludes everything, doesn't it?

This chapter was a great experience to reflect on the lives of widows and widowers that have influenced or touched my life in some significant way. It is interesting to me what we tend to remember about people, and hopefully that is true of my life as well. Do we want people to remember us fondly? Or will they remember us for the negativity in our lives?

Each of the women and men that I have tried to portray accurately (though I took some writer's liberty with my grandmothers) touched my life in some way. Yet, each touched me in different and unique ways. Except for my grandparents, I met everyone else at church. Many of those I included have passed on, and so I write this in honor of their lives. I hope that their family members will accept these words as a memorial to their lives.

Maria T.

Of all the widows I have honored and have influenced my life, Maria is the reason that I traveled to Portugal five times between February 2015 and June 2016. Maria was Brazilian born, raised by a Catholic single mother, and did not know her father. She has the distinction among all the widows that I have written about, to have been widowed at a very young age. She was married for approximately 45 days in her early 20s when her husband died of a massive heart attack. Unknown to both of them was that he possessed a genetic condition.

To characterize Maria as being in a state of confusion and grief at such a young age, would be an understatement. She would testify that by the mercy of the Lord, she survived all the options and distractions of life, to find Jesus. She would also testify that God is not only a father to the fatherless, He is a Husband to the husbandless.

I classify our relationship as serendipity, a true God-planned appointment. The first time I flew to Portugal, I arrived at SeaTac airport in Seattle with my brother-in-law, Glenn, only to discover at check-in that I had grabbed my expired passport. I quickly called Glenn with the dilemma, and he came back to pick me up. We quickly drove to my apartment an hour away in Everett, secured my current passport, and returned to SeaTac literally five minutes after cutoff for baggage check-in. United found a flight on Alaska to get me to my connecting flight in Newark. I was all checked in and only had to check my baggage. Well, the lines were long!

Of all days, Alaska was training new agents, and the lines were incredibly slow. The result was that I missed my flight. They wanted another $150, and they couldn't guarantee that I would get out until the following Monday. This was a Saturday, and I only had a total of 10 days for my trip. I thanked them and ran back to United and explained my situation. They got back online and found me a flight with Lufthansa to Frankfurt, then Lisbon and on to Faro. I would leave at 2 pm and get to my destination by 11:30 Sunday evening, 12 full hours later than I was originally scheduled to arrive; but that was better than losing another two to three days and a surcharge.

The bottom line...God's sovereignty was all over the trip. I stayed with her pastor, Michael Findlay, and his wife Yoka. I met many of Maria's friends and established friendships that will be for life. Maria also showed me many beautiful beaches and countryside. To underscore God's provision and sovereignty, on my return trip back through Newark, I learned that the weekend before, 3,000 flights had been canceled. I believe that I would have been stuck in Newark. God had rerouted me over the storms on the east coast and delivered me to my destination all without any additional surcharge. God opened my eyes to the needs of widows internationally and provided several opportunities for ministry on my various trips to Portugal.

CHAPTER 5

THREE MOST IMPORTANT WIDOWERS IN THE BIBLE

I know that the title "Most Important" is relative, but for my purposes I mean these men are positionally important to the lineage of Christ. They are considered forefathers of the Hebrew nation, and thus critical to the line leading to Christ. We do not find the word widowers in the Bible.

I think we don't see the term because the established order ordained by God is that the man is the provider and caretaker of his wife. I find it interesting that the terms widow and widower are only found in context to a married relationship. In today's culture in the U.S., we have some states that recognize what is called common law marriage, meaning that if a couple has lived together in a committed relationship for seven years or longer, these certain states will recognize the couple as being married. Again, the terms are only found in a married relationship. We don't just call someone a widow or widower without being legally married.

Abraham

An important widower noted in the Bible is Abraham. We are told in Gen. 23:1-2 that Sarah lived "one hundred and twenty-seven years; and Sarah died in Kiriath-arba, that is Hebron, in the land of Canaan." Abraham mourned for Sarah and wept for her. Abraham was grieving his loss of a long-term marriage to Sarah.

We are told that Abraham asks for "a burial site...that I may bury my dead out of sight." The response from the sons of Heth, "Bury your dead in the choicest of our graves; none of us will refuse you his grave for burying your dead." Abraham was given a "field and a cave, which was deeded over to Abraham for the price of four hundred shekels of silver, commercial standard." (Gen. 23:4-20) He honored Sarah with a distinguished burial, purchasing the choicest property that he could acquire.

So, why is it important to recognize Abraham's wife? I think it says something important about Abraham and his love for Sarah (princess), that he honored her life. We see a man that is heartbroken over the loss of Sarah. The writer of Genesis spares us no detail to emphasize that Abraham wept.

Men listen up. It is okay to show emotional pain in the form of tears. If there is one thing that I have held against my dad, it is that I have never seen him cry over loss. One of the things that I will always remember about my dad, however – and he is still living – is that he can laugh so hard that he cries through the laughter watching cartoons. As a child, I mentioned that we used to watch Looney Tunes cartoons, especially the Road Runner and Wile E. Coyote.

The name Abraham means "father of multitudes." He is considered the first Hebrew patriarch, and he became known as the prime example of faith. Abraham's life is crucial, for from his relationship with God and Sarah comes a covenant promise of a son. Both Abraham and Sarah were old – 100 and around 90, respectively – when Isaac was born.

But it is crucial to understand the events that preceded Isaac's birth. Neither Abraham nor Sarah believed the promise of God. In fact, Sarah "laughed" when she heard. It all seemed preposterous to her. One of the monumentally bad choices in all of history was conceived when Abraham took the advice of his wife Sarah, and went into Hagar and she conceived and birthed Ishmael.

After the death of Sarah, Abraham sought a bride for Isaac. A woman named Rebekah was obtained from Abraham's relatives in

Mesopotamia, and Isaac married her gladly (Gen 24:67). In fact, it says that "Isaac loved her…and was comforted (by Rebekah) after his mother's death.

We are told that Abraham in old age remarried and had additional children, dying at the age of 175 years. More widowers remarry than widows; in fact, most widows over the age of 60 do not remarry. God Himself was known subsequently as the God of Abraham (Exodus 3:6). Through him God had revealed His plan for human salvation (Exodus 2:24). The promises became assurances for future generations (Exodus 32:13; 33:1). Abraham became known as "God's friend forever." (2 Chron.20:7)

Jacob

The next widower that I want to introduce to you is Jacob. He is a very interesting man raised in a dysfunctional family. His family seemed to major in deception. Jacob means "he grasps the heel" or "he cheats, supplants." Gen. 25: 26, 27:36

Isaac and Rebekah are barren, and Isaac prays to the Lord on behalf of his wife, and the Lord answered him, and Rebekah conceived. But the children struggled together within her, and she said, if it is so, why then is it this way? So, she went to inquire of the Lord. And the Lord said to her, "Two nations are in your womb; and two peoples shall be separated from your body; and one people shall be stronger than the other; and the older shall serve the younger."

Now that sets the stage for sibling rivalry from the get-go, and the kids do not disappoint. Reading on, "When her days to be delivered were fulfilled, behold, there were twins in her womb. Now the first came forth red, all over like a hairy garment; and they named him Esau. And afterward his brother came forth with his hand holding on to Esau's heel (aptly named?) and his name was called Jacob." Esau we are told became a skillful hunter, but Jacob was a peaceful man, living in tents. We are told that each parent had a favorite (Isaac loved Esau, and

Rebekah loved Jacob), already a recipe for disaster and something that all parents need to avoid.

Well, as the boys grow, we are told that a day comes when Esau comes home famished, and finds his brother Jacob with a pot of a stew-like concoction. Esau in a moment of poor judgment feels that he is going to die anyway if he doesn't get something to eat right now, parts with his birthright for a temporary meal. It was after he had eaten that he came to his senses and realized he had made a grave mistake. The text says, "Esau despised his birthright."

Then sometime later, a day comes when Isaac proclaims to Esau that the day of his death is approaching, and he should go out and hunt game and "prepare a savory dish for his father." But Rebekah overhears and quickly tells Jacob to put skins on his arms and go into his dad pretending to be Esau, deceive his father, and steal the blessing of Esau for himself. Isaac had Jacob come close; he smelled like Esau and felt like Esau even though the voice wasn't an exact match. Thus, Jacob stole the blessing from his brother.

Things like that just don't make for future goodwill in the family. Well, fast forward to Jacob on the run landing in Haran, the land of his uncle Laban. Jacob meets Rachel and the sparks fly, and Jacob agrees to work seven years for Rachel. He works the seven years that seem "but a few days because of his love for her (Gen. 29:20)." But Laban has other plans, and after too much wedding celebration Leah is sent to the tent instead of Rachel. We are not told how Rachel felt about that turn of events; but it is no secret who Jacob prefers, and we see a great case of why sister wives don't work.

Laban covers his deception by saying that it is not their custom for the younger to marry first. So, Jacob agrees to work another seven years, but has to only wait one more week before taking Rachel as his second but preferred wife.

God sees the dynamic, and opens and blesses Leah's womb with the first four boys, causing great jealousy for Rachel because she cannot conceive. Between Rachel and Leah and their handmaidens, Bilhah and Zilpah, they have a collective 12 boys, who become the 12 tribes of Israel. Joseph was the eleventh son born to Rachel. She later has a second son for Jacob whom she names Ben-oni (son of my sorrow), and Jacob calls him Benjamin (son of the right hand). Rachel dies while giving birth to Benjamin. (Gen. 35:16-20)

Again, we see a widower after losing his wife, honor her by doing something that would create a long-term memorial, erecting a "pillar over her grave." Jacob, for all his wrestling with God and deception in his relationships with his family, was used of God to father the nation of Israel. In fact, his name was changed from Jacob to Israel ("God strives"; "God rules"; "God heals"; or "he strives against God"). Gen. 32:28; 35:10 NASB

Ezekiel

Never would I have thought to consider the man Ezekiel, but he became a widower following a conversation with Adonai Ezekiel 24: 15-18 & 27b: "The word of Lord came to me saying: Son of man, behold, I am about to take from you the desire of your eyes with a blow. But you shall not mourn, and you shall not weep, and your tears shall not come. Groan silently; make no mourning for the dead. Bind on your turban , and put your shoes on your feet, and do not cover your moustache, and do not eat the bread of men. So, I spoke to the people in the morning, and in the evening my wife died. And in the morning, I did as I was commanded....Thus you will be a sign to them, and they will know that I am the Lord." (Ezekiel 24: 15-18 & 27b NASB)

Emotions for men can be difficult and the era that I was raised in created confusion. Big boys don't cry. I don't want to disparage my dad but I recall him saying to me, you better stop crying or I'll give you something to cry about. Dad did believe in corporal punishment and I had a healthy respect for my dad.

In the past seven years there has been a transformation in my life regarding crying. Many times at worship or when a specific song comes on the radio, my heart can become so full of the Spirit, I become overwhelmed and the tears flow. One thing that Ezekiel prophesied was that ADONAI would give his people a *new heart*, "And I shall give them one heart, and shall put a new spirit within them. And I shall take the heart of stone out of their flesh and give them a heart of flesh, that they may walk in My statutes and keep My ordinances, and do them. Then they will be My people, and I shall be their God. (Ez. 11:19-20 NASB)e

The Spirit of God and the Word of God transforms us. Together they create a love for God and for people. Apart from God and the Word, we cannot hope to fulfill the new covenant. Without a new heart and a new mind (Ro. 12:2b) we cannot hope to transformed. Without transformation we will never see the peoples that God wants us to see.

We are not told that Ezekiel struggled to maintain over the loss of his wife. He just states the facts, that "in the morning I did just as I was commanded." I believe that he was sustained by the Spirit.

In the few years that The Widows Project has been in operation, I have sat in on numerous grief support classes that we provide. I have heard their stories, widow and widower alike and they tell of the deep loss, grief and loneliness that they experience. I have seen those come to class newly widowed, and all they can do is weep and cry during the entire class. The pain is so raw. Ezekiel is an exception and not the rule.

Research shows that the widower in particular is at a much higher risk for suicide than their married counterpart and older males at even higher risk (Suicide after Bereavement—An overlooked Problem, Commentary from F1000, Henry Brodaty; Adrienne Withall; Medscape Nov. 1, 2019).

At The Widows Project, we find that 80% of the support that our widowed members need is of the emotional variety. That is why we started with a grief support group and then have advanced to a women's

(Circle of Friends) and men's group (Circle of Strength) for social support, a greeting card line called Heartfelt Cards – a resource for pastors, friends & family – and then in January 2020 we will launch Side by Side, a seminar that equips widows who have already traveled the road of grief, to emotionally come alongside those new to widowhood. They will be equipped to take the comfort they have received from God according to 2 Cor. 1:3-4, and pass it along to the new widow.

CHAPTER 6

WHAT IS PURE?

I n the book of James, we find a verse that is often quoted, but is it understood? It says, "This is pure and undefiled religion in the sight of our God and Father, to visit orphans and widows in their distress, and to keep oneself unstained by the world."

I think that if we want or desire to make proper application of this verse, we must have an understanding of what James is telling us. Do we really want to please God? Do we want to offer up a pure and undefiled worship to God? Do we define religion in the same terms that Jesus defines religion? Do we value what He values? Is what He finds important, what we find important?

Let's define "pure" or "purity" first. According to The Holman Illustrated Bible Dictionary (Brand, Draper, & England, 2003), "The primary Hebrew root word for pure (tahar) often refers to pure or flawless gold (1 Kings 10:21; Job 28:19; Ps. 12:6). Tahar and other Hebrew words for "pure" are used to describe other objects such as salt (Exod. 30:35), oil (Exod. 27:20), and incense (Exod. 37:29). Thus, a basic Old Testament meaning is that of "refined, purified, without flaw, perfect, clean" (cp. Lam. 4:7).

In the Old Testament (OT), there was the act of "ritual purity" that was to be performed by His people with a priest in preparation to worship God. Purity qualified one to participate in worship, an activity central to the life of ancient Israel. One could not come into His presence and be unclean — either by being in contact with a disease, emission, a deceased animal, or person. Even the priests had to purify themselves, the altar, and the instruments used in sacrifice to God.

Each family had to have their own animal for their sacrifice, which was determined by their social class. The poor were allowed to substitute less valuable animals for use in their sacrifices. "Ethical Purity" was also important to God. Thought and behavior befitting the people of God are pure (Ps. 24:4; 73:1; Prov.15:26; 22:11; 30:12). Such purity of thought is to result in conduct which is appropriate for people (Ps. 119:9; Prov. 16:2; 20:9, 11; 21:8).

Psalm 15 gives us a description of a citizen of Zion [which was used as synonymous with Jerusalem as the city of David, or the city of God in the new age (Isa. 1:27; 28:16; 33:5), or to the heavenly Jerusalem (Isa. 60:14; Heb. 12:22; Rev. 14:1)], the place where the Messiah would appear at the end of time. The psalmist mentions character that "walks with integrity, and works righteousness, and speaks truth in his heart. He does not slander with his tongue, nor does evil to his neighbor, nor takes up a reproach against his friend; in whose eyes a reprobate is despised, But who honors those who fear the Lord; He swears to his own hurt and does not change; He does not put out his money at interest, nor does he take a bribe against the innocent. He who does these things will not be shaken."

It sounds to me like we could use a dose of this character today in America. It is important not to distinguish sharply between ritual and ethical purity in the OT. God expects ethical purity, and sin results in uncleanness. Thus, sin and ritual uncleanness stand together in the OT as unacceptable to the Lord.

Since the OT assumes that people are going to encounter sin and uncleanness, it provides a way to return to cleanness. There was use of waiting periods where the contaminated one was quarantined for a specific waiting period while he/she was observed, and then at the end of the waiting period was examined. If they didn't have a scab or infection any longer, they were given a clean bill of health by the priest.

If they still showed some sign of uncleanness, then the quarantined time was extended.

A cleansing agent was required: water, blood, or fire (Num. 31:23). Water was the most common purifying agent. Blood was used to cleanse the altar and the holy place (Lev. 16:14-19).

The final element of the ritual of purification is sacrifice. Purification from discharges required two pigeons or turtledoves, one for a sin offering and one for a burnt offering (Lev. 15:14-15, 29-30). The priest also touched the person's extremities with blood from the offering and with oil, cleansing and life-renewing agents.

In the New Testament (NT), uses of words for purity relate to cleanness of some type. Old Testament meanings are often reflected. Perfection is the meaning in Mark 14:3; this is mixed with religious purity in Heb. 10:22; 1 John 3:3.

Ethical purity dominates in the NT. The person who is in right relationship with God is to live a life of purity (2 Tim. 2:21-22; Titus 1:15 and references to a pure heart- Matt. 5:8; 1 Tim. 1:5; Heb. 9:14; James 4:8; 1 Pet. 1:22). Purity is also listed among virtues (2 Cor. 6:6; Phil. 4:8; I Tim. 4:12, Mark 7:15).

I think that James is challenging us to examine our motives. Notice that just verses before vs. 27 that he says, "Be doers of the word and not hearers only." Actions support what you say you believe. We can say that we believe in the support of the widow, the orphan or the poor, but until we actually do it, do we really believe it? Why do we not seek the highest forms in expression of our faith?

Today's culture is giving a lot of emphasis on eating organic and avoiding foods that are tainted by pesticides, steroids or growth hormones. Perhaps it is time that we as a faith community seek what is "pure" expressions of our faith. Seek to serve those who He says should have our compassion and by so doing, we are doing to Him.

CHAPTER 7

KINGDOM CARE

S orrowfully, it has taken me years to finally engage in the social gospel and the needs of my community.

I applaud the faith-based organizations that have taken on the prison ministries (which we don't hear as much about anymore). I applaud those who have taken on the issues of orphans, poor children, inner city children, adoption, families, the abused and battered, single parent families. I applaud those who have taken on the neglected or disparaged, such as those with Alzheimer's, addictions, and sex trafficking.

I am sure that I have missed somebody in trying to recognize the scope of work that is going on. What do the various groups have in common? We have heard the expression, "The squeaky wheel gets the grease!" Most of these groups are loud and highly publicized. We see them daily on the nightly news or late night television. We see the highly emotional and highly effective ad campaigns that draw our attention to the pain and suffering that each group is experiencing.

Yet, I tell you: There is one more group that needs our help. They don't draw attention to themselves. They don't act out with violence, hold rallies or protests; yet their pain and suffering is real.

I see in the Scriptures one more class of people that Jesus calls attention to that has virtually been ignored. Most would use or quote James 1:27; but I want to introduce this people with other Scripture, because I think it draws attention to the invisibility of this group, too.

For I believe that until we put a face and skin on this people, we will not notice them. Please join me as we take a look at Matthew 25:31-46:

31 "But when the Son of Man comes in His glory, and all the angels with Him, then He will sit on His glorious throne.

32 All the nations will be gathered before Him; and He will separate them from one another, as the shepherd separates the sheep from the goats;

33 and He will put the sheep on His right, and the goats on the left.

34 "Then the King will say to those on His right, 'Come, you who are blessed of My Father, inherit the kingdom prepared for you from the foundation of the world.

35 For I was hungry, and you gave Me something to eat; I was thirsty, and you gave Me something to drink; I was a stranger, and you invited Me in;

36 naked, and you clothed Me; I was sick, and you visited Me; I was in prison, and you came to Me.'

37 Then the righteous will answer Him, 'Lord, when did we see You hungry, and feed You, or thirsty, and give You something to drink?

38 And when did we see You a stranger, and invite You in, or naked, and clothe You?

39 When did we see You sick, or in prison, and come to You?'

40 The King will answer and say to them, 'Truly I say to you, to the extent that you did it to one of these brothers of Mine, even the least of them, you did it to Me.'

41 "Then He will also say to those on His left, 'Depart from Me, accursed ones, into the eternal fire which has been prepared for the devil and his angels;

42 for I was hungry, and you gave Me nothing to eat; I was thirsty, and you gave Me nothing to drink;

43 I was a stranger, and you did not invite Me in; naked, and you did not clothe Me; sick, and in prison, and you did not visit Me.'

44 Then they themselves also will answer, 'Lord, when did we see You hungry, or thirsty, or a stranger, or naked, or sick, or in prison, and did not take care of You?'

45 Then He will answer them, 'Truly I say to you, to the extent that you did not do it to one of the least of these, you did not do it to Me.'

46 These will go away into eternal punishment, but the righteous into eternal life." (NASB)

There is much to mention about this passage as Jesus addresses the topic of the judgment of the nations. He administrates this judgment first by nation, and then He separates everyone into two groups: sheep and goats. The sheep represent the faithful Jewish remnant and those who are "regenerated", born again by the blood of the Lamb (Jesus), and will proclaim the gospel of the Kingdom in all the world. Notice that the proclamation includes care for the physical needs of the unsaved in the form of food, drink, and clothes. "For I was hungry, and you gave Me something to eat; I was thirsty, and you gave Me drink; I was a stranger, and you invited Me in; naked, and you clothed Me; I was sick and you visited Me" (vs. 35).

Allow me to say, one cannot be a stranger if he is already in the Kingdom of God. In the verse preceding vs. 35 Jesus says, *"Come, you who are blessed of My Father, inherit the kingdom prepared for you from the foundation of the world."* Where are the sheep seated? They are seated at the right hand of Jesus, at the position of privilege. One does not "inherit" anything unless you are related by birth! Not in the physical world, nor in the spiritual world.

In a parable in Luke 14:16-24, Jesus tells us of a "certain man" that was giving a dinner, and the man invited many but for various reasons "many" did not come. Since there was still room at the table for more, he exhorted his "slave", "Go out into the highways and along the hedges, and compel them to come in, that my house may be filled."

I don't know of a more compelling way to bring someone into the Kingdom than to marry the Gospel of Jesus with the provision of the physical needs of mankind. Jesus knew this was the key from the foundation of the world. It has taken me years to come to this place of conviction, and this is why The Widows Project was launched. The evangelical must be joined to the social gospel of provision.

This is why we must be an advocate for the needs of widows because they have silently, invisibly suffered for too long. Like the Parable of the Good Samaritan, we have failed widows by omission. We have just walked by them without seeing or acknowledging the need. The ironic thing is that these are your grandparents, your uncles and aunts, and even perhaps your brothers or sisters. Occasionally, they are your children. They are our biological family. Let's draw them into the Kingdom, if they aren't already. Let's "compel" them, which is to "strongly urge" them to come to the table!

CHAPTER 8

HOW GREAT IS THE NEED

Statistics are of great value and even God included the use of numbers in the Bible. Even one of His books is titled, Numbers. Yet, while God seems to give significance to numbers, He gives more importance to the value of people than mere numbers.

According to the U.S. Census Bureau, the national total widow population stood at 19.6M (Elliott & Simmons, 2011). If we take that figure and add approximately 1.5 million per year, every year since 2012, we begin to approach our total widowed population. The numerical difference between widow and widower is consistently two to one, which documents what we already know, that women tend to outlive their spouses two-thirds of the time.

The numerical data is good news for those of us who want the supportive data that any business with good sense would require. If there is a substantiated need and the numbers show demand, then logic would suggest that the potential financial return is more than adequate to support a business aimed at any group of people. However, numbers in the Kingdom of God are not the primary motivating factor, nor should they be.

God is motivated by value! I don't even want to attempt some great theological discourse to support this statement. Suffice it to say, there are several scriptural references that would provide biblical support; none greater than John 3:16 as stated by God through Jesus, "For God so loved the world, that He gave His only begotten Son, that whoever believes in Him should not perish, but have eternal life." Please notice that "world" encompasses every people, of every nation; no exceptions, limitations, or numerical restrictions.

Further biblical evidence from the mouth of God is witnessed in the Luke 15 parable about the lost sheep. Listen as Jesus says, "What man among you, if he has a hundred sheep and has lost one of them, does not leave the ninety-nine in the open pasture, and go after the one which is lost, until he finds it?" How much more so with people?

Well, God addresses this question in Matthew 6: 25-26 "For this reason I say to you, do not be anxious for your life, as to what you shall eat, or what you shall drink; nor for your body, as to what you shall put on. Is not life more than food, and the body than clothing? Look at the birds of the air, that they do not sow, neither do they reap, nor gather into barns, and yet your heavenly Father feeds them. Are you not worth much more than they?" God not only establishes value, He assumes responsibility for man; "He feeds them," and ascribes "worth."

Remember the Widow of Zarephath? In paraphrase we are told that she, her son, and the prophet Elijah, were all providentially provided for. God sustained them, and they survived the drought! Again, we see the intimate, providing nature of God. HE is concerned about the smallest and least of the details. He saw that nameless widow and met her need.

How do these examples apply to us? If we believe that the Bible is applicable to us today, how can we not ask ourselves the tough questions? How can we not give the same value to the widowed among us? How can we not apply the same level of care? Do we care about the things that Jesus cares about? Do we really understand that when we do for those that cannot care for themselves and cannot pay back benevolence extended to them, that we have done it unto and for Jesus? Can we any longer walk past them without seeing?

What I seek to accomplish in writing this book is to make the invisible, visible. I want to advocate for their help so that we can no longer walk past them. I aim to start in my Jerusalem before I go into the Puget Sound region, then Washington State, the nation, and to the uttermost parts of the world. I understand that there is great need, and perhaps even greater need in other parts of the world.

But I believe that God has given us the blueprint at the instituting of His Church in Acts 1:8, "But you shall receive power when the Holy Spirit has come upon you; and you shall be my witnesses both in Jerusalem, and all Judea and Samaria, and even to the remotest part of the earth." The model is established for us. Start in your Jerusalem and then spread out. All are of equal value. We need not ignore, overlook, or demean any who are disadvantaged.

The Holy Spirit tells us in the Book of James, that caring for the widow and orphan are "pure religion." Let's take Him at His word and seek the purest and true in our lifestyle of worship before God. We cannot care and serve without humility. This is the very character of God as manifest in Jesus, "who humbled Himself." We may pray and say we want to be like Christ, but unless true humility is embraced, we won't truly care and serve.

This is why I have come to the conclusion that the issue of the poor, the orphaned, and the widowed is a Kingdom government issue and not a human government issue. We dare not get relaxed and give over the responsibility of the disadvantaged to the government. If we truly ascribe to be of His Kingdom, then the responsibility is ours in alliance with God and not our earthly government. When we take responsibility in cooperation and obedience to God, then we will see change in our communities, our nation, internationally, in one another, and ourselves. It starts with me and then begins with us.

I believe that The Widows Project is my "do." For years, I realize that I didn't get it. It has taken me a lifetime of sermons and personal Bible study, but the penny finally dropped. I hope that it doesn't take you a lifetime as it did me. I could no longer walk on by and treat the widowed as if they were invisible and didn't matter. I hope that you will join me in caring and serving the widowed of our city, our county, our region, state, and nation. To the widowed, I want to say that I am sorry that I wasn't here for you sooner. To the Church, we can do no less now that we know. They are waiting for us. Will you join me?

CHAPTER 9

LOST RESOURCE

I sn't it a wonderful thing to discover new teachings in the Bible that have perhaps been archived and lost over the centuries to the local Church? Or, perhaps, certain instructions have been ignored and easier to walk by rather than address. Or, does the lack of implementation signal the overall state of the Church and the family unit in today's society? The question begs to be asked, "Is this teaching still applicable to the Church today?

What I am about to share with you is not my own discovery, and I'll give credit to Dr. John MacArthur (1986) for his teaching on the topic of I Timothy 5:1-16. His teaching gave light to a passage that I had never understood or at least paid little attention. As a quick observation, I find it interesting that this passage follows a chapter on "overseers and deacons", a section on "apostasy", and an exhortation to the young man Timothy on "godliness" as a discipline of those who minister. Additionally, the instruction concerning "elders" at the end of this chapter continues to develop the theme of the leadership of the early church.

We know from letters written by Paul that Timothy was raised in the faith and taught by his "grandmother Lois and his mother Eunice" (2 Tim. 1:5). There was a generational transfer of "sincere faith" to Timothy. He was a product of the product at the hands of godly mothers. Is it possible that both Lois and Eunice were widows, as we have no mention in this passage of a father's presence? Is this part of the reason that Paul seems to take on a "fatherly" role instructing young Timothy? Were Lois and Eunice already modeling the teaching and instruction of Paul to the women and mothers of the early Church?

I am primarily going to focus on the concept of a "list" that Paul twice references in verses 9 and 11, and the qualifications that are given for being placed on "the list." These are widows that are defined as "widows indeed" — a term that is mentioned three times (vs. 3, 5, & 16). What does Paul mean by a "widow indeed?" It seems that he is telling us that she is first identified by the absence of a man and more specifically a husband in her life. She has no support in the financial and familial areas of life as evidenced in verse 4.

Paul evaluates on the basis of the presence of "children or grandchildren" as having frontline responsibility for her care. We honor our parents by fulfilling the fifth commandment (Ex. 20:12) in this manner. It is a return on the investment that grandparents and parents have made in pouring themselves into our lives as children. They sacrificed for us. We, in turn, are to be a primary support when those times like widowhood arrive.

In fact, Paul goes deeper to say that if we find ourselves in the position of having the ability and the opportunity to support a widow in our own family and we do nothing, we "have denied the faith, and is (are) worse than an unbeliever." This is strong language about our obligation. It is our "do" and something that our society continues to distance itself from. Perhaps it is time for us as a community of faith to take a serious look at our role to the widow.

The picture that Paul gives a "widow indeed" is one who has "fixed her hope on God, and continues in entreaties and prayers night and day." This widow is what I call an "Anna." In a previous chapter, I spoke about a widow, Anna, who was privileged to observe the dedication and consecration of Jesus by a devout man named Simeon in the temple. She had only been married for seven years when her husband died; and then for the continuation of her life, she "never left the temple, serving night and day with fastings and prayers" (Luke 2:37).

This is the type of devoted character that Paul is speaking about. This woman is totally devoted to God as her new husband and provider. She has no interest or desire in remarriage. It is interesting that Paul uses the age of 60 as a cut-off. Even the national statistics — including all widows, whether of faith or not — give evidence that the highest percentage of widows 60 and older will live alone (Widow's Hope, 2016).

So, this draft is a list of requirements that Paul gives us for a "widow indeed" to be on "the list."

1. **60+ years old**: This may not be a hard line of demarcation but serves for the purpose that the "widow indeed" needs to possess a high level of maturity physically and spiritually. If the physical desire for a man is not completely fulfilled, then it is prudent that she not be on the list. To be less would have implications that Paul later addresses regarding widows who should not be on the list. He provides plenty of reasons "why" they do not belong on the list. They sound like today's reality television chaos. It is important that just like the Church maintains scriptural requirements for elders, deacons, and pastors we uphold the standard for ministry by widows to the Church. And it is with these standards that we give additional honor and support to those who exemplify godliness.

2. **A one-man woman**: This is a topic that used to be hotly debated. Let us agree that the issue here is primarily one of being a woman whose heart, commitment, and devotion is exclusive to one man at a time. The highest standard would be one man for a lifetime. I have met women who have been widowed more than once. They remarried and outlived two or three men. They would be penalized for taking this statement to the extreme.

3. **A reputation for good works**: This statement sounds much like the qualification of an elder or overseer as proposed in I Tim. 3:7, "And he must have a good reputation with those outside the

Church." If individuals do not have a good reputation living their lives out before the community at large, they are going to cause disrespect for the Church. We do not need any person in leadership to be living a double standard lifestyle. It causes the name of Christ to be brought into disrepute. By contrast, imagine the tremendous benefit to the Church to have as a resource widows that possess these characteristics.

4. **Brought up children**: Who better to teach young women about children and relationships to their husbands than a mature, godly widow. There is a saying that I think most of you have heard that says, "You don't know what you've got until it's gone." Not only have these widows experienced children leaving the home, but in losing a husband they probably have a higher value on what they lost when they lost their spouse. My hunch is that they will give the young mother a paradigm of appreciation and respect that a man desires. She also may provide much needed motherly guidance and support that some women may have never received from their own mothers. What value can we place on the role that a widow like this would bring to the Church?

5. **Shown hospitality to strangers**: Heb. 13:2, "Do not neglect to show hospitality to strangers, for by this some have entertained angels without knowing it." I believe that hospitality is a gifting, and this "widow indeed" to be on "the list" is to possess this gift.

6. **Assisted those in distress**: She has a heart for those who are disadvantaged, helpless, and hopeless. She possesses the Father's heart and understands that by her doing for those in this position, she is doing it to Jesus (Matt. 25:34-46). Her actions flow from a heart that is owned by God. Love is the mark of the Christian as expressed in John 13:34-35. It is a marker, an identification that identifies us as distinctly belonging to Christ. The world responds to true love. But then, don't we all!

7. **Devoted to every good work**: The text has already shown that the focus of this particular widow that is to be included on "the list" is totally focused on the kingdom and the King of all Kings. Her purpose in life is a total submission to Jesus. She no longer possesses a desire for a man, nor the things of this world. This is the widow who belongs on this list.

I mentioned a widow in my chapter on those have influenced my life that had this gift. She made everyone feel included and embraced, and most of her hospitality was around a meal. Most of the meals were not extravagant "I-spent-all-day-in-the-kitchen" type of affairs. They were extensions of her heart toward everyone because of her heart for Jesus. She was also an encourager. How many times to I remember her consoling someone else and inviting them to stay and enjoy a meal. She also took people in that needed a place to stay short-term. Most were young people that were from another sate and away from family. Her place at times looked like a revolving door or musical chairs: "Who is staying at your home today?" She truly believed that her home was provided by God, and she used it as a resource for the kingdom.

What a difference it makes in our lives when we know whose we are, that all we have comes from Him, and then we offer everything back to God for His use. What have we forfeited in not being hospitable to those we come in contact with?

She washed the saints' feet: I hope that you have participated in the experience of washing someone else's feet. It is an extraordinary and humbling experience. I have been both the washer and the receiver of being washed. When it is done in sincere humility, you will be moved with compassion for the person you are washing. Even the pose that is required is an act of humbling oneself and attending to the need of another. This was perhaps not a ceremony like we tend to make it. Because this act is not part of our culture, it tends to be a heightened experience.

In the Jewish culture, it was a subservient act conveying respect and love. According to the Holman Illustrated Bible Dictionary (Brand, Draper, & England, 2003):

"Footwashing was regarded as so lowly a task that it could not be required of a Hebrew slave. Jesus' washing of the disciples' feet (John 13:4-5) has both an ethical and a symbolic sense. The ethical sense is emphasized in John 123:14-15 where Jesus presented Himself as the example of humble, loving service (Luke 22:27). The command to do for one another what Christ had done for them ought not to be confined simply to washing feet. What Jesus did for the disciples was to lay down His life for them (John 15:13). Thus, the ethical imperative calls for giving our lives in extravagant acts of selfless service. Footwashing is one expression of this. (p. 592)."

Washing the feet of saints is one of the qualifications given to the Church for a widow to be on this list.

My focus in this chapter was to raise awareness about the apparent existence of a "list" in the early Church. A list that points to a special group of widows that ministered to the widows, the women and children of the early Church. This passage raises a lot of questions such as:

- Where has this ministry gone?
- Why did it disappear?
- What kind of value would a group of widows like this group bring to the Church today?
- What church would reevaluate their ministry in light of this instruction given by Paul and reorganize their priorities?
- What value would it bring to the family life of the Church?
- How would today's Church implement a ministry group like this?
- Does this form of ministry apply to today's culture?
- Are we wasting a vital resource through omission?

I hope your hearts have been stirred and challenged to consider our responsibilities to the widow and her role in the kingdom. It is much larger than I could have imagined and more vital than we have valued. My concern for a long time has been that the widowed are underserved and undervalued. They tend to be invisible and dishonored. We have walked past them without noticing them long enough.

The Widows Project purposes to serve both the widow and the widower with the love of Christ because it is a traumatic event for either partner to lose a long-time spouse. When Jesus expresses in the Beatitudes, "Blessed are those who mourn, for they shall be comforted," He didn't qualify between the man and the woman. He didn't differentiate between cultures or denominations. Grief is universal. There may be differences in levels of help and kinds of help, but we seek to meet the emotional and spiritual needs of both in hopes that they will see Jesus in us.

A 21-DAY DAILY DEVOTIONAL

Developing the Father's Heart for the Widowed

TWP Guidelines for Journal Section

The Journal Section follows the format Wayne Cordeiro (2008) uses in The Divine Mentor: Growing Your Faith as You Sit at the Feet of the Savior.

- Title
- Scripture
- Observations
- Application
- Prayer

It is my hope that you will read each passage and allow the Holy Spirit to speak to you. If you have never attempted to study the Bible, I recommend getting a copy of The Divine Mentor: Growing Your Faith as You Sit at the Feet of the Savior by Wayne Cordeiro (2008). He not only provides you with the "why" of doing your own inductive, daily journaling time with God, but also supplies you with examples like the fourteen that I have selected below.

- Please consider reading the passage listed below each title, meditating on it, and writing out a short observation of what it was communicating to you.
- Then make a personal application stating what kind of action you will now take based on what you have just read.
- Write a short prayer.
- Continue on through Day 21 with the passages for each day.

The last seven days are passages that have been discussed in the book and allow you to gain additional insight beyond what I shared. I pray that God will create in you a heart for the widowed, and join us in serving the widowed in your neighborhood, state, region, and our nation.

DAY 1

A WIDOWED AND DISGRACED PRINCESS

Lamentations 1

Title: A Widowed and Disgraced Princess
Scripture: Lamentations 1: 1-2

> *1 How lonely sits the city that was full of people!*
>
> *She has become like a widow*
>
> *Who was once great among the nations!*
>
> *She who was a princess among the provinces*
>
> *Has become a forced laborer!*
>
> *2 She weeps bitterly in the night*
>
> *And her tears are on her cheeks;*
>
> *She has none to comfort her*
>
> *Among all her lovers.*
>
> *All her friends have dealt treacherously with her;*
>
> *They have become her enemies. (NASB)*

Observations:

Since God has placed on my heart the plight of widows, this first verse of Lamentations caught my eye this morning. The author of Lamentations (most likely Jeremiah), compares Zion (Jerusalem) to someone who is widowed and as a disgraced princess. He pictures this widow as one who "weeps bitterly in the night" and is so despondent that "her tears (flow) on her cheeks." Apparently, everyone has left her isolated and alone, for there is "none to comfort her." Even her "little ones", her children, have abandoned her.

In verse 12, the hopelessness is so great that all she can lament is the greatness of her pain, "Look and see if there is any pain like my pain!" By verse 16, she is totally consumed by her sorrows, and she begins to go through a mental list of her misfortunes. "For these things I weep; My eyes run down with water; Because far from me is a comforter, One who restores my soul; My children are desolate because the enemy has prevailed." She wonders if she can continue, the weight of her burden is so great that she concludes, "For my groans are many, and my heart is faint." This is too much to bear!

I believe that there are many widows in our communities that are suffering silently. They are overwhelmed with the loss of their spouse and the enormity of facing life without them. Can we help? Or do we continue to respond like the "priest" and the "Levite", or do we act like the "good Samaritan?" Jesus asks us, "Which one was the neighbor?" He didn't stop in the Luke passage with just the question that He poses to us. Once we answer, Jesus tells us, "Go and do the same" (Luke 10:36-37).

Application:

I will do the same and found The Widows Project.

Prayer:

Father, You have great love for people and great compassion for the poor and disadvantaged. In the first chapter of Lamentations, You focus on the widow, comparing the calamity of Zion (Jerusalem) to that of a widow. Help me to help them. Don't allow them to suffer in obscurity and alone. I pray this in Jesus' name. Amen.

DAY 2

THE WIDOWS' GIFT

Luke 21:1-6

Title: The Widow's Gift
Scripture: Luke 21:1-6

1And He looked up and saw the rich putting their gifts into the treasury.

2And He saw a poor widow putting in two small copper coins.

*3And He said, "Truly I say to you, this poor widow
put in more than all of them;*

*4for they all out of their surplus put into the offering; but she out of her
poverty put in all that she had to live on."*

*5And while some were talking about the temple, that it was adorned with
beautiful stones and votive gifts, He said,*

*6"As for these things which you are looking at, the days will come in which
there will not be left one stone upon another which will not be torn down."*

(NASB)

Observations:

Yet another time that we observe Jesus using a widow to illustrate a point. He was watching people of all walks, with various financial abilities, and speaking to His disciples. He drew their attention to what was really going on right in front of them. For Jesus, being God, knew the intentions of the heart (1 Chr. 28:9, Heb. 4:12).

According to the text she was "poor" and gave out of her "poverty", while the "rich" were giving out of "their surplus." Her giving took faith; their giving required no faith. They knew that they had more to draw from where that came; she "put in all that she had to live on." She was relying on God for survival; they were relying on themselves. Her giving was painful; their giving was pain-free.

I think that we can draw not only the personal comparisons from the participants, but also, if we look closer, there is more wisdom, a deeper wisdom to consider. Notice that Jesus not only draws the disciples' attention to the giving, as well as the motives and intentions of the heart, but Luke points out to us details about the conversations of some who "were talking about the temple."

I have had the pleasure of visiting some cathedrals in Europe (specifically Portugal), and it is natural when touring sites to take in the architecture and how the structure is adorned with gold, stone and stained glass windows. One cathedral that I visited had a designated room that housed a number of centuries-old, highly ornate vestments, crowns and jewelry of the former clergy.

This passage points to the paradox of man and his misdirected attempts to honor God in complete indifference to what God tells us to us to do in order to bring Him honor. We tend to invest in structures. Jesus invested in man. I find it ironic that God is preparing a place for His people, and it will be adorned with the most majestic precious stones that man can imagine. But, do you notice that even gold is used for asphalt in the New Jerusalem? God does not honor what we honor even in His kingdom.

Application:

This message is for the true kingdom of God.

Prayer:

Father, I (we) have done it wrong for so long. Forgive my lack of understanding and not hearing You. I am listening. Help me to share this message for Your kingdom and to Your true followers. I pray this in Jesus' name. Amen.

DAY 3

THE HEART OF GOD

Psalm 68:5-6; 146:9

Title: The Heart of God
Scripture: Psalm 68: 5

> 5 *"A Father of the fatherless and a judge for the widows,*
> *Is God in His holy habitation." (NASB)*

Observations:

At the time of this writing, considering that The Widows Project is in the final stages of obtaining the 501c3 designation, the reading of this passage was extremely timely. I am going to focus on the relationship of God to widows. It is interesting to me that God is not only a "Father of the fatherless", but He is specifically characterized as a "judge for the widows." What is a judge's role in the Old Testament? It is an official with authority to administer justice by trying cases.

For example, Moses served as the judge of Israel, both deciding between persons and teaching Israel God's statutes (Exod. 18: 15-16). At Jethro's suggestion, Moses himself served as the people's advocate before God and their instructor in the law (18: 19-20), and appointed subordinate judges to decide minor cases (18:21-23). Elders of a community frequently served as judges at the city gate (Deut. 22:15; 25:7; Job 29:7-8). Difficult cases were referred to the priests or to the supreme judge (Deut. 17:8-13). During the monarchy, the king served as the supreme judge (2 Sam. 15:2-3) and appointed local judges (1 Chron. 23:4; 2 Chron. 19:5).

Complaints against judges are frequent in the OT literature. Absalom took advantage of discontent with the legal system to instigate revolt (2

Sam. 15:4). Judges are accused of showing partiality (Prov. 24:23) and of taking bribes (Isa. 10:2; Jer. 5:28). Zephaniah described the judges of Jerusalem as wolves on the prowl (3:3).

God is the ultimate Judge of all the earth (Gen. 18:25; Isa. 33:22; James 4:12). What we see in God that supersedes what we see in man is that God is absolutely just. He cannot be bought or be accused of showing partiality. He has no agenda other than to be consistent with and to His nature. So, God is an advocate, a protector, and a judge for widows.

Application:

Just as God is a judge (advocate/protector/provider) to widows, so shall I be.

Prayer:

Father, may my heart be just like Yours. Not just concerned but embraces empathy that results in action. People are suffering in silence and we have the resources to aide and benefit widows across this nation. Help us to help them. I pray this in Jesus' name. Amen.

DAY 4

YOU HAVE TURNED MY MOURNING INTO DANCING

Psalm 30:1-4; 10-12

Title: You Have Turned My Mourning into Dancing! or Joy Comes in the Morning!
Scripture: Psalm 30: 1-4; 10-12

1 I will extol You, O Lord, for You have lifted me up,

And have not let my enemies rejoice over me.

2 O Lord my God,

I cried to You for help, and You healed me.

3 O Lord, You have brought up my soul from Sheol;

You have kept me alive, that I would not go down to the pit.

4 Sing praise to the Lord, you His godly ones,

And give thanks to His holy name.

10 "Hear, O Lord, and be gracious to me;

O Lord, be my helper."

11 You have turned for me my mourning into dancing;

You have loosed my sackcloth and girded me with gladness,

12 That my soul may sing praise to You and not be silent.

O Lord my God, I will give thanks to You forever. (NASB)

Observations:

God has been gracious to me and my family. My parents are still living, as are aunts and uncles. Death has not touched my family closer than my grandparents, who I didn't know well, as they lived in the Midwestern United States.

I have always wondered what do people do without the Lord? The rough answer is that they despair. There is little hope scripturally that a pastor can give those whose loved one has died apart from a relationship with the Lord.

David addresses a place known as "sheol" in this psalm. Sheol is a place that his culture and generation would understand well because it was known as the "place of the dead", or more specifically, the place of the unrighteous dead according to the Hebrew Bible. Sheol occurs 21 times in "psalmodic" type literature; 20 times in "reflective" literature; 17 times in prophetic literature; and eight times in narrative literature (Brand, Draper, & England, 2003, p. 1483).

Sheol in the OT is roughly analogous to hades in the NT. Hades is that realm set over against God and His righteous kingdom — the dwelling place of the unrighteous and their "king." Then we find at the end that death and hades are cast into the lake of fire (Rev. 20:14). The final destiny of those who dwell in sheol/hades is eternal separation from God's righteousness and love. As they sought to be separate from Him in life, so will they be in death and in eternity.

This is why David is able in the 139th Psalm to say: 7 "Where can I go from Thy Spirit? Or where can I flee from Thy presence? 8 If I ascend to heaven, Thou art there; If I make my bed in Sheol, behold, Thou art there." He could not flee from God's presence. Jonah could not flee from God's presence, either by means of a boat or the depth of the sea in the belly of the great fish. That is why Paul is able to say, "Who shall separate us from the love of Christ?", and say "nothing." Absolutely, nothing, nothing!

Hope is only found in Jesus. Notice the words above. If you sought separation from Christ on earth, so will you be in death and in eternity.

It is your choice. If you have chosen Christ and chosen life in and through Him, then you have eternal life in and with Him. It is more than baptism or a prayer. If you have chosen Him, then walk with Him in His presence. You will experience what David experienced, "Joy comes in the morning," because "Thou hast turned for me my mourning into dancing; Thou hast loosed my sackcloth and girded me with gladness; That my soul may sing praise to Thee, and not be silent. O Lord my God, I will give thanks to Thee forever." (Ps. 30: 11-12 NASB)

Paul additionally adds these words in 1 Thess. 4: 13-18 "13 But we do not want you to be uninformed, brethren, about those who are asleep, so that you will not grieve as do the rest who have no hope. 14 For if we believe that Jesus died and rose again, even so God will bring with Him those who have fallen asleep in Jesus. 15 For this we say to you by the word of the Lord, that we who are alive and remain until the coming of the Lord, will not precede those who have fallen asleep. 16 For the Lord Himself will descend from heaven with a shout, with the voice of the archangel and with the trumpet of God, and the dead in Christ will rise first. 17 Then we who are alive and remain will be caught up together with them in the clouds to meet the Lord in the air, and so we shall always be with the Lord. 18 Therefore comfort one another with these words." (NASB)

Application:

I will declare the gospel of salvation.

Prayer:

Father, how glorious is Your name in all the earth. I have hope because Jesus has declared salvation to me a sinner that was condemned and unclean. I confess with my mouth that Jesus is Lord, and that I choose life in Him. For years, I lived thinking that my sin was not so bad and not as bad as others. But, when I finally took an honest assessment of my life, I found that I had been deceiving myself; and that I needed to confess my sin, ask for forgiveness and turn from my wicked ways and follow You, Lord. I have hope and joy. I look forward to serving You and finishing the race strong. I pray this in Jesus' name. Amen.

DAY 5

WIDOWS INDEED

I Timothy 5:1-16

Title: Widows Indeed
Scripture: 1 Timothy 5: 3, 5, and 16

> *3 Honor widows who are widows indeed.*
>
> *5 Now she who is a widow indeed, and who has been left alone has fixed her hope on God, and continues in entreaties and prayers night and day.*
>
> *16 If any woman who is a believer has dependent widows, let her assist them, and let not the Church be burdened, so that it may assist those who are widows indeed. (NASB)*

Observations:

The word "indeed" is defined:

> *adverb - in fact; in reality; in truth; truly (used for emphasis, to confirm and amplify a previous statement, to indicate a concession or admission, or, interrogatively, to obtain confirmation):*
>
> *Indeed, it did rain as hard as predicted.*
>
> *Did you indeed finish the work?*

Paul is instructing us and a young Timothy how to identify a widow "indeed." One who is "in fact; in reality; in truth; truly" a widow is characterized as one who "has been left alone (her spouse has passed), has fixed (placed) her hope (fully) on God, and continues in entreaties and prayers night and day." She is by definition in today's terms a prayer warrior.

This is the widow as defined by Paul that is deserving of Honor. He doesn't tell us how to honor her, but we are told to give her "honor." We are also told that if we have a "widow" who is a "dependent" of ours, that we are to provide her care and not to "burden" the Church. This implies not only an individual responsibility, but also implies that the "Church" has a responsibility.

It is my belief that the Church has ignored or shirked that responsibility, and has given it to the government. When we do that, there is always a price associated with that decision. Either we embrace the social gospel with an attitude of doing it as unto the Lord, or we secure the oppressive nature of the government and their growing definition of social government. We have a responsibility either way.

Application:

I prefer to carry the gospel to the needy in Jesus' name!

Prayer:

Father, I have many lessons to learn. It has taken me a lifetime, and I still don't have them all down. I'm just now learning some to which I have been oblivious. Help me as I learn. I pray this in Jesus' name. Amen.

DAY 6

TO THIS WIDOW ONLY

Luke 4:14-26

Title: To This Widow Only
Scripture: Luke 4:25-26

> *25 But I say to you in truth, there were many widows in Israel in the days of Elijah, when the sky was shut up for three years and six months, when a great famine came over all the land;*
>
> *26 and yet Elijah was sent to none of them, but only to Zarephath, in the land of Sidon, to a woman who was a widow. (NASB)*

Observations:

Jesus is referencing the account in 1Kings 17:8-16, "The word of the Lord came to him, saying, Arise, go to Zarephath, which belongs to Sidon, and stay there; behold, I have commanded a widow there to provide for you." So, he arose and went. Elijah was sent to a widow that had no means to supply his needs, and God establishes Himself as a Father to the fatherless and a Husband to the widow.

The text says that there was in the land a famine that was caused by the "sky (being) was shut up for three years and six months," and states that "there were many widows in Israel in the days of Elijah," but that he "was sent to none of them, but only to Zarephath, in the land of Sidon, to a woman who was widow." He was sent to this widow only. The key seems to be the preceding verse (24) "And He (Jesus) said, Truly, I say to you, no prophet is welcome in his hometown." Unbelieving and unreceptive hearts kept God from working among the people in that land.

Application:

Keep your heart receptive to the inner working of God.

Prayer:

Father, may it never be said of me that You were not able to work in me because of unbelief and an unreceptive heart. For I know that anyone who comes to You must come in faith. Because without faith it is impossible to please You. According to Hebrews 11: 6, "I must believe that You are God, and You are a rewarder of those who seek You." I pray this in Jesus' name. Amen.

DAY 7

LOOK WHO ATTENDED JESUS' DEDICATION

(You can miss her if you are not paying attention!)

Luke 2:21-38 (key 36-38)

Title: Look Who Attended Jesus Dedication
Scripture: Luke 2:36-38

> *36And there was a prophetess, Anna the daughter of Phanuel,
> of the tribe of Asher. She was advanced in years and had
> lived with her husband seven years after her marriage,*
>
> *37and then as a widow to the age of eighty-four. She never
> left the temple, serving night and day with fastings and prayers.*
>
> *38At that very moment she came up and began giving thanks to
> God, and continued to speak of Him to all those who were
> looking for the redemption of Jerusalem. (NASB)*

Observations:

Have you ever been in the right place at the right time? I recall years ago in about 1976 that I traveled to Southern California to look at a college and have some vacation. Unknown to me the day I traveled to Disney Land; an important dignitary was anticipated to visit. Helicopters were flying overhead; masses of press correspondents were being led through the complex; swat teams were on the roofs of various stores; and the daily parade was being delayed. Who was making an appearance that warranted that kind of attention? We discovered it was the Emperor of Japan. We got just a brief glance as the security moved him thru the parade.

Imagine how blessed and honored Simeon felt...but there was another servant of God that was watching and beholding the glory of God. Her name was Anna, a "prophetess…advanced in years…and a widow." Who would ever think that someone that had never left the temple, "serving night and day with fasting and prayers," would ever be privileged to see the promised Messiah? Simeon was promised to see the "consolation of Israel." Anna was not. But she was in the right place at the right time, and "began giving thanks to God, and continued to speak of Him to all those who were looking for the redemption of Jerusalem." The Holy Spirit inspired Luke to include a small passage that recognized a widow for eternity by making mention of her attendance at this holy ceremony of dedicating Jesus, and her response of "giving thanks" and "telling everyone" who was looking for the Messiah.

Application:

Widows are significant to God. He does not overlook them.

Prayer:

Father, thank You for noticing what the world considers insignificant. Those that are considered insignificant by the world (widows, orphans, the poor) are significant to You! Likewise, they should be significant to us and cared for by us. With Your help, we will take on the responsibility of caring for the widows. I pray this in Jesus' name. Amen.

DAY 8

SURPLUS & POVERTY

Mark 12:41-43

Title: Surplus and Poverty
Scripture: Mark 12: 41-43

> *41 And He sat down opposite the treasury, and began observing how the people were putting money into the treasury; and many rich people were putting in large sums.*
>
> *42 A poor widow came and put in two small copper coins, which amount to a cent.*
>
> *43 Calling His disciples to Him, He said to them, "Truly I say to you, this poor widow put in more than all the contributors to the treasury;*
>
> *44 for they all put in out of their surplus, but she, out of her poverty, put in all she owned, all she had to live on." (NASB)*

Observations:

I love this account by Mark that describes Jesus observing "how the people were putting money into the treasury." The contrast is between two extremes, one rich and one poor; one who gave it all, and the others who didn't give an equal sacrificial gift. It is like that story of the chicken and the pig. Both were asked to contribute something towards a breakfast meal. The pig replied, "It is easy for you to say, let's make a contribution. For me it is a sacrifice, and for you it is a donation." This woman, Jesus says, "put all she owned, all she had to live on." She gave it all. The poor widow had what I would call extreme faith. Where is your faith in contrast?

Application:

Start exercising extreme faith today.

Prayer:

Father, You need more people like the poor widow who will exercise extreme faith. May I begin to be counted among the extremely faithful. I pray this in Jesus' name. Amen.

DAY 9

I SEARCHED FOR A MAN:
HONOR WIDOWS INDEED

Title: I Searched for a Man & They Did Not Repent
Scripture: Ezekiel 22: 23-31 & Revelation 9: 20-21

23 And the word of the Lord came to me, saying,

24 "Son of man, say to her, 'You are a land that is not cleansed or rained on in the day of indignation.'

25 There is a conspiracy of her prophets in her midst like a roaring lion tearing the prey. They have devoured lives; they have taken treasure and precious things; they have made many widows in the midst of her.

26 Her priests have done violence to My law and have profaned My holy things; they have made no distinction between the holy and the profane, and they have not taught the difference between the unclean and the clean; and they hide their eyes from My sabbaths, and I am profaned among them.

27 Her princes within her are like wolves tearing the prey, by shedding blood and destroying lives in order to get dishonest gain.

28 Her prophets have smeared whitewash for them, seeing false visions and divining lies for them, saying, 'Thus says the Lord God,' when the Lord has not spoken.

29 The people of the land have practiced oppression and committed robbery, and they have wronged the poor and needy and have oppressed the sojourner without justice.

30 I searched for a man among them who would build up the wall and stand in the gap before Me for the land, so that I would not destroy it; but I found no one. 31 Thus I have poured out My indignation on them; I have consumed them with the fire of My wrath; their way I have brought upon their heads," declares the Lord God. (NASB)

Revelation 9: 20-21

> *20 The rest of mankind, who were not killed by these plagues, did not repent of the works of their hands, so as not to worship demons, and the idols of gold and of silver and of brass and of stone and of wood, which can neither see nor hear nor walk;*
>
> *21 and they did not repent of their murders nor of their sorceries nor of their immorality nor of their thefts. (NASB)*

Observations:

In Ezekiel, we see that "the word of the Lord" made emphasis on the corruptness of the leadership of the land, the "prophets", "her priests", and "her princes." In fact, the corruptness was so severe that "her prophets" is mentioned a second time, saying that they are saying "thus says the Lord God, when the Lord has not spoken."

And just as we see in Genesis a conversation between Abraham and the Lord, are there any righteous in the land? (Genesis 18: 16-33) God and Abraham had a conversation about the "outcry" of Sodom and Gomorrah, and if God destroyed Sodom and Gomorrah, would He also not destroy some righteous people, too? So, how many righteous people would it take for God to relent and have mercy on Sodom and Gomorrah? Abraham started with 50, and God was willing to relent. However, Abraham reassessed the situation and didn't feel secure that God would find 50, so he kept reducing the number of righteous until he was down to 10. The question we need to ask ourselves is, are we one of the 10 that is keeping God's wrath at bay for our city, and ultimately our country? In both Ezekiel and Revelation, the answer is the same: verse 30a, "I found no one," and "they did not repent."

Application:

I will be the man who will 'build up the wall and stand in the gap before God for the land."

Prayer:

Father, I recall Isaiah's vision in chapter 6 where he says, "Woe is me, for I am ruined! Because I am a man of unclean lips, and I live among people of unclean lips; For my eyes have seen the King, the Lord of hosts." Verse 8, "Then I heard a voice of the Lord saying, Whom shall I send and who will go for Us?" Then I said, "Here am I. Send me." I asked to be used of You Father. Prepare the way and the hearts as they hear the vision of The Widows Project. In the name of Jesus, I pray. Amen.

DAY 10

SCRIBE ALERT

Title: Scribe Alert
Scripture: Luke 20: 45-47

> *45 "And while all the people were listening, He said to the disciples,*
>
> *46 'Beware of the scribes, who like to walk around in long robes, and love respectful greetings in the market places, and chief seats in the synagogues, and places of honor at banquets,*
>
> *47 who devour widow's houses, and for appearance's sake offer long prayers; these will receive greater condemnation.'" (NASB)*

Observations:

Again, we are quoted by Luke a warning by Jesus, "Beware of the scribes." Who are the scribes? According to Holman Bible Dictionary, scribes were "persons trained in writing skills and used to record events and decisions" (Jer. 36:26; 1 Chron. 24:6; Esther 3:12) (Brand, Draper, & England, 2003, p. 1452). During the exile in Babylon, educated scribes apparently become the experts in God's written word, copying, preserving, and teaching it. Ezra was a scribe in the sense of being an expert in teaching God's word (Ezra 7:6). A professional group of such scribes developed by NT times, most being Pharisees (Mark 2:16). They interpreted the law, taught it to disciples, and were experts in cases where people were accused of breaking the Law of Moses. They led in plans to kill Jesus (Luke 19:47) and heard His stern rebuke (Matt. 23).

So, why did Jesus warn us about the scribes? It was because of attitudes and actions. I believe it was because they were the religious experts of the day who had much influence and as such, they loved to be noticed; they loved position and prestige; and they loved to exercise power over the weak and disadvantaged. The abuse was so egregious that Luke uses a description like he is speaking of lions, hyenas, great white sharks, or killer whales: They "devour widow's houses!"

We currently mention "predatory lending" in our nation, but Jesus is speaking of those who take wealth and property by stealth after someone of disadvantaged ability becomes husbandless. No one looking at these scribes would believe that they were capable of such deeds, but the action stems from the heart; and Jesus announces, "These will receive greater condemnation." Let this serve as a warning to those with the disposition to defraud others (especially widows), and help us to be on the lookout and protect the widowed from such people.

Application:

We (I) have a responsibility to warn others of the words of Jesus and build a directory of business leaders who will serve the widowed ethically, morally, and with compassion.

Prayer:

Father, I am your slave and I am listening to Your Son! Thank you for the alert! In the name of Jesus, I pray. Amen.

DAY 11

PRESSING NEEDS

Title: Pressing Needs
Scripture: Titus 3: 14

> *14 And let our people also learn to engage in good deeds to meet pressing needs, that they may not be unfruitful. (NASB)*

Observations:

As the President of The Widows Project, my hope is that not only will we seek to meet practical needs, but also that we might also be able and willing to meet pressing needs as we are able. The distinct difference is that practical implies day-to-day needs that would enhance the quality of daily life; but pressing encompasses urgent, critical needs. Pressing needs may include paying a bill so that water and heat are not shut off; or an urgent medical or dental procedure is needed; or someone is homeless and hungry. I like the way Paul addresses Titus and us to consider doing more where there is need.

Application:

I will lead TWP as we have the means to consider doing more for the widows and widowers who have pressing needs.

Prayer:

Father, I can never out-give you. You are the giver of every good and perfect thing, and You challenge me to give "cheerfully", for You "love a cheerful giver" (2 Cor. 9:7). Thank You, Father, for the seed which You supply; and promising to "supply and multiply" the seed that will be sown in Your name. I want TWP to be a ministry like Paul speaks of in this chapter, "For the ministry of this service is not only fully supplying the needs of the saints, but is also overflowing through many thanksgivings to God." Bless those who are going to give to the establishing of TWP, and for the abundance of partners that together with You produce an overflow. Along with Paul, I say, "Thanks be to God for His indescribable gift!" In the name of Jesus, I pray. Amen.

DAY 12

HE KEPT GIVING

Mark 6:33-52 (key vs. 41 & 52)

Title: He Kept Giving…
Scripture: Mark 6: 30-44

> *30 The apostles gathered together with Jesus; and they reported to Him all that they had done and taught.*
>
> *31 And He said to them, "Come away by yourselves to a secluded place and rest a while." (For there were many people coming and going, and they did not even have time to eat.)*
>
> *32 They went away in the boat to a secluded place by themselves.*
>
> *33 The people saw them going, and many recognized them and ran there together on foot from all the cities, and got there ahead of them.*
>
> *34 When Jesus went ashore, He saw a large crowd, and He felt compassion for them because they were like sheep without a shepherd; and He began to teach them many things.*
>
> *35 When it was already quite late, His disciples came to Him and said, "This place is desolate, and it is already quite late;*
>
> *36 send them away so that they may go into the surrounding countryside and villages and buy themselves something to eat."*
>
> *37 But He answered them, "You give them something to eat!" And they said to Him, "Shall we go and spend two hundred denarii on bread and give them something to eat?"*
>
> *38 And He said to them, "How many loaves do you have? Go look!" And when they found out, they said, "Five, and two fish."*

39 And He commanded them all to sit down by groups on the green grass.

40 They sat down in groups of hundreds and of fifties.

41 And He took the five loaves and the two fish, and looking up toward heaven, He blessed the food and broke the loaves and He kept giving them to the disciples to set before them; and He divided up the two fish among them all.

42 They all ate and were satisfied,

43 and they picked up twelve full baskets of the broken pieces, and also of the fish.

44 There were five thousand men who ate the loaves.

Observations:

First of all, I want to declare (in years past we used to say "testify" of…) my love for the Word of God. For I find in the Word daily encouragement and strength to follow Him and live a lifestyle of obedience to Him. It is my hope that those reading this will likewise find daily solace, strength, and hope in God's Word!

There is much to glean from today's text; so, while I am not going to go verse by verse in an exhaustive exegesis of this text, I want to give emphasis to the highlights. So, let's get started. Notice first of all, that I didn't select my text based on the division of the Bible's translators into nice, neat subject breaks. Rather, I chose to tie together what I believe has significance to this passage and to our lives today.

This passage starts out by saying that "the apostles gathered together with Jesus; and they reported to Him all that they had done and taught." What is this referring to? Mark cannot be referring to the immediate verses preceding, from 14-29, because this is all about John the Baptist's death. Mark has to be tying this passage to the passage of vs. 7-13 where Jesus is sending out the "twelve…in pairs…giving them authority over the unclean spirits;" and instructing them about their ministry journey, what to take and how to comport themselves. This passage concludes with, "and they went out and preached that men should repent. And they were casting out many demons and were anointing with oil many sick people and healing them." After giving their report, Jesus said, "Come away by yourselves to a lonely place and rest a while."

I believe that this is a word for every follower of Jesus, but especially those that are leaders and workers in the kingdom. We have to recharge ourselves not only by the daily intake of God's Word; but also, we are restored and recharged when we purposely seek a secluded place to be with God! Notice in vs. 31 that added in brackets is the statement ("For there were many people coming and going, and they did not even have time to eat.") If there are two things that I hear from so many pastors, they are, "I am tired," and "I don't have time to ….. (and you fill in the blank…there is a plethora of answers)." We find many accounts of Jesus going to a secluded place (a garden, a mountain) to be alone (and away from busy-ness and people). If you are a leader in and among His sheep, you can do no less!

So, after being restored and recharged, we are told that "Jesus went ashore, He saw a large crowd, and He felt compassion for them because they were like sheep without a shepherd; and He began to teach them many things." He didn't go ashore before he was restored and recharged. But, when He did go ashore, "He saw a large crowd, and He felt compassion for them because they were like sheep without a shepherd." The usage of the analogy "people being like sheep" is used by Jesus as a visual concept with which His listeners would be familiar, since their culture was largely based around flocks and herds of sheep.

Shepherds' main purposes were to watch over (protection and safety); to feed them (by moving them to pastures); to care for them (sheering them, health maintenance); and to provide leadership (unifying them as a herd). People, too, become scattered spiritually, without under-shepherds. The Church needs leadership provided by under-shepherds who are compassionate (seeing people the way Jesus sees them) and teach them as Jesus did in this account.

What did Jesus teach them? We are not told, but we do know what He was teaching His disciples. It was getting late in the day and, "His disciples came up to Him and began saying, The place is desolate (there are no markets or restaurants or even drive thru fast food options) and it is already quite late; send them away so that they may go into the surrounding countryside and villages and buy themselves something to eat."

How do you interpret the disciples' concern? Are they genuinely concerned but are not willing to do anything personally about this dilemma? Are they just clueless and do not realize that the "Bread of Life" is standing right before them? So, what is Jesus' response? "You give them something to eat!" Can you imagine the look on the disciples' faces? They must have been thinking, "Are you kidding us?" Notice how they question Jesus. "Shall we go spend….two hundred denarii (a day's wages) on bread and give them something to eat?"

Let's pause there to say: Is this not the first thing that we ask when we have been charged with the task of feeding God's sheep? There was a story that I heard years ago about a pastor who was in a new pastorate, his first Sunday on the job, and he decided to get a reading on how well his congregation knew the Bible (Cybersalt Consulting and Communications, 1998-2017). So, where else do you start but with a Sunday School primary class of seven-year-olds.

Some of you probably remember a segment from The Linkletter Show [1952-1970], "Kids Say the Darndest Things," so you know what is coming (IMDb.com, Inc., 1990-2017).

So, the pastor visited Mrs. Armstrong's class. She acknowledged the new pastor and was all excited that he would want to come visit her class. He thanked her and told her that he would like to spend a few minutes talking with the kids. She was delighted and told him that she had a few administrative things to do; so, she told him that his visit was perfect timing, and that this would allow her to complete her paperwork and take it down to the education director's office. So, off she went, and the pastor sat down in the circle of seven-year-old children.

He introduced himself and then told the children that he had a very important question to ask them, and that he wanted them to be very honest with him! Okay? …They all agreed. So, the pastor paused and said, "Boys and Girls, who tore down the walls of Jericho?" They all began looking at one another; several became scared and finally one little boy named Billy n jumps up and declares, "I don't know, and I didn't do it!"

At that moment, Mrs. Armstrong entered the room, and the pastor walked over to her and asked her to step out in the hall for a moment. Full of concern, he relayed the story to Mrs. Armstrong saying, "I told the kids that I was going to ask them a very important question, and that I wanted them to be very truthful with me." They assured me that they would be truthful. So, I asked them, 'Who tore down the walls of Jericho?' After a few moments of silence, and all of them frantically looking around at each other, Billy jumped up and emphatically declared, 'I don't know, and I didn't do it!'"

Mrs. Armstrong reached over to the pastor's arm, patted it, and said, "Pastor, I've known little Billy since he was born. I'm a personal friend of his parents; and if Billy said that he didn't do it, then he didn't do it!"

About that time, the educational director came by and entered the discussion. The pastor told him that he had taken a moment to get acquainted with the kids in Mrs. Armstrong's class, and that he had sat down in the circle and told that boys and girls that he wanted to ask them a very important question and wanted them to be very honest with him, to which they all agreed. So, I asked them, "Boys and Girls, who tore down the walls of Jericho?" After several moments of silence and all of them frantically looking around at each other, Billy jumped up and emphatically declared, "I don't know, and I didn't do it!"

To which Mrs. Armstrong responded, "I've known little Billy since he was born. I'm a personal friend of his parents; and if Billy said that he didn't do it, then he didn't do it! The educational director rolled his eyes and said to the pastor, "Pastor, it doesn't matter who tore down those walls. Let's go to the director of finance, and we will get enough money to rebuild those walls!"

Can you imagine? Well, he learned a lot about his congregation that day. This illustrates the importance of teaching the sheep how to feed themselves spiritually.

Application:

On a higher note, what did Jesus teach His disciples right before their very eyes? His first question was, "And He said to them, 'How many loaves do you have? Go look!' And when they found out, they said, 'Five, and two fish.' Jesus asked them essentially, what do you have? What resources are already available to you? "Go look!" He asked them to assess the situation and they found out that had "Five (loaves), and two fish."

The disciples, along with us, would look at that situation and say, "Lord, it looks hopeless!" Our treasury is low, and we have already blown our budget...by my calculations Lord, at $5 per happy meal we need $25,000 just to feed the men — and that's without tax and a tip! So, Jesus showed them that nothing for Him was too difficult.

The Scripture says, "He took the five loaves and the two fish, and looking up toward heaven, He blessed the food and broke the loaves and"...and a miracle happened. "He kept giving and giving and giving and giving....and they ate and were satisfied!" Jesus took what they had..."blessed" it...meaning He offered to God something (food in this example), and He asked God His Father to make the object (food) a source of blessing for others! He did this in front of them as an example of how they themselves should ask for a blessing from the Father for the benefit of others.

God is the source of everything and a blessing too. Right before their eyes, Jesus called out to God (Jehovah Jireh, My Provider), and provided from little to blessing; all "were satisfied" and beyond (they picked up twelve baskets of the broken pieces, and also of the fish)." Twelve baskets of both bread "pieces" and fish "pieces"…from five loaves and two fishes."

I know, the non-believing are saying, "Not possible." They are looking up Jesus' sleeves and in the refrigerators behind Him!

The believing are saying, "That's My God!"

Would God have been glorified by running to the market? God is God; by doing what is impossible to man and for man to do! In fact, if you want to boggle your mind, look at Genesis 1 with understanding. God "created" the earth out of waste and emptiness. I hear the unbelieving, "It's not possible!"

Or take a look at Genesis 2, how God "formed man of dust from the ground, and breathed into his nostrils the breath of life; and man became a living being." And later in the chapter, "And the Lord God fashioned into a woman the rib which He had taken from the man, and brought her to man."

I know; I hear the unbeliever's crying, "Not possible." With man, you are correct. But my Bible says, "With men this is impossible, but with God all things are possible. (Matt. 19:26). Do you know the definition of the word possible? Possible means: that which can exist. So, my fellow followers of Jesus, in the future let us take what can exist and ask God to bless it so that what is impossible can become supernaturally possible. What a great lesson for all of us to learn! This is a most relevant lesson for our spiritual family, if we desire to make our spiritual life in Christ a faith lifestyle today.

Prayer:

Father, I show my faith in You when I ask for something that is impossible for me alone to accomplish. I ask for Your help in forming, establishing, creating, founding, staffing, and funding The Widows Project. In Jesus' name. Amen.

DAY 13

THE HELPLESS...DO YOU WANT TO BE BLESSED?

Psalm 41 (key vs. 1-3)

Title: The Helpless...Do You Want to Be Blessed?
Scripture: Psalms 41: 1-3

> *1 How blessed is he who considers the helpless;*
> *The Lord will deliver him in a day of trouble.*
>
> *2 The Lord will protect him, and keep him alive, And he shall be called*
> *blessed upon the earth; And do not give him over to the desire of his enemies.*
>
> *3 The Lord will sustain him upon his sickbed; In his illness,*
> *Thou dost restore him to health. (NASB)*

Observations:

This psalm is directly attributed to David and begins with a promise to those who have a heart for "the helpless." He states, "How blessed is he who considers (to give thought that acts) the helpless;" for there will be direct benefits from the Lord. This person will experience "deliverance in a day of trouble;" he will receive protection; he will be spared (kept alive); he will be "called blessed upon the earth;" he will not be taken captive and he will be sustained (long-term care without interruption) and restored (returned to excellent health). It appears to me that this is the kind of favor that I desire from my Heavenly Father.

Before we continue this day, let's define with the help of Scripture those who are "the helpless."

Ezekiel 16: 49: "Behold, this was the guilt of your sister Sodom: she and her daughters had arrogance, abundant food, and carless ease, but she did not help the poor and needy."

James 1:27: "This is pure and undefiled religion in the sight of our God and Father, to visit orphans and widows in their distress…"

Matt. 25:35-36: "For I was hungry, and you gave Me something to eat; I was thirsty, and you gave Me drink; I was a stranger, and you invited Me in; naked, and you clothed Me; I was sick, and you visited Me; I was in prison, and you came to Me."

There are more examples — like the Scripture where God says He will be a Father to the Fatherless — but I think we understand that "the helpless" by definition are those who can't help themselves, defend themselves, feed themselves, or care for themselves. Additionally, they can't return the help that you extend them. It is the type of giving that God gave us in Romans 5:6-8, "For while we were still helpless, at the right time Christ died for the ungodly. For one will hardly die for a righteous man; though perhaps for the good man someone would dare even to die. But God demonstrates His own love toward us, in that while we were yet sinners, Christ died for us."

Did you catch that? We were "helpless" when Christ died for us. We could not help ourselves because we had no righteousness in ourselves. So, Jesus did for us what we could not do for ourselves. If we have received His grace, we now have His righteousness and His character. If we have His Spirit, we now have the power to be His agents of love and compassion to the helpless.

Application:

In obedience, I must care for the helpless.

Prayer:

Father, helping the helpless is nothing more and nothing less than being ambassadors of Jesus to those who cannot help themselves. I have a responsibility to those who are helpless. Help me to fulfill my responsibility in love and compassion. In Jesus' name I go. Amen.

DAY 14

YOU COMFORT US SO THAT WE CAN COMFORT OTHERS

II Corinthians 1:1-11

Title: You Comfort Us So That We Can Comfort Others
Scripture: 2 Cor. 3-11

3 Blessed by the God and Father of our Lord Jesus Christ, the Father of mercies and God of all comfort,

4 Who comforts us in all our affliction so that we will be able to comfort those who are in any affliction with the comfort with which we ourselves are comforted by God.

5 For just as the sufferings of Christ are ours in abundance, so also our comfort is abundant through Christ.

6 But if we are afflicted, it is for your comfort and salvation; or if we are comforted, it is for your comfort, which is effective in the patient enduring of the same sufferings which we also suffer;

7 And our hope for you is firmly grounded, knowing that as you are sharers of our sufferings, so also you are sharers of our comfort.

8 For we do not want you to be unaware, brethren, of our affliction which came to us in Asia, that we were burdened excessively, beyond our strength, so that we despaired even of life;

9 Indeed, we had the sentence of death within ourselves so that we would not trust in ourselves, but in God who raises the dead;

10 Who delivered us from so great a peril of death, and will deliver us, he on whom we have set our hope. And He will yet deliver us,

11 You also joining in helping us through your prayers, so that thanks may be given by many persons on our behalf for the favor bestowed on us through the prayers of many. (NASB)

Observations:

Who can comfort like Christ? No one! Who can comfort us like one who has gone through what you are going through in Christ? Another widow or widower? If we have suffered and experienced the comfort of Christ in our life, whatever the area of suffering, as a follower of Jesus we are uniquely qualified to walk alongside those who are "sharers of our suffering" and become "sharers of our comfort."

When we are sharers of the same faith in the same God, we mutually share a faith and confidence that God "will deliver us" and that fellow believers will also "join in helping us through (their) your prayers, so that as you are delivered and comforted, thanks may be given by many persons on (your) behalf for the favor (of God) bestowed on us through the prayers of many."

I believe that this is why we need to enroll and serve as many Christ-believing widows and widowers so that they may experience a comfort that the world does not experience. And upon their testimony of comfort and deliverance from fear, anxiety, hopelessness, and loneliness that other widows and widowers will be won to Jesus!

Application:

No one understands like Jesus, and no one understands like someone who has walked where you have walked and experienced comfort.

Prayer:

Father, what a powerful message that You have given through Paul. You are the great deliverer and comforter, and we are blessed that we too can share our comfort and hope with others. Help us build a community that comforts those who need comforting and hope. In Jesus' name. Amen.

DAY 15

ELIJAH, A WIDOW SHALL PROVIDE FOR YOU!

Title: Elijah, a Widow Shall Provide for You!
Scripture: I Kings 17:8-24

Observations

Application

Prayer

DAY 16

WHAT IS A MOABITESS?

Title: What is a Moabitess?
Scripture: Ruth 1 & 2

Observations

Application

Prayer

DAY 17

WHAT IS A REDEEMER?

Title: What is a Redeemer?
Scripture: Ruth 3

Observations

Application

Prayer

DAY 18

WHO IS RUTH TO KING DAVID? A ROYAL LINE!

Title: Who is Ruth to King David? A Royal Line!
Scripture: Ruth 4

Observations

Application

Prayer

DAY 19

WHAT IS IN A GENEALOGY? WHO IS RUTH TO JESUS?

Title: What Is in a Genealogy? Who is Ruth to Jesus?
Scripture: Matthew 1:1-17

Observations

Application

Prayer

DAY 20

AM I A SHEEP OR A GOAT?

Title: Am I a Sheep or a Goat?
Scripture: Matthew 25:31-46

Observations

Application

Prayer

DAY 21

IF THIS IS THE HIGHEST OR BEST, HOW CAN I DO ANY LESS?

Title: If This is the Highest or Best, How Can I Do Any Less?
Scripture: James 1:27

Observations

Application

Prayer

REFERENCE CHART

Adult Stress Scale

Adults

To measure stress according to the Holmes and Rahe Stress Scale, the number of "Life Change Units" that apply to events in the past year of an individual's life are added and the final score will give a rough estimate of how stress affects health.

Life event	Life change units
Death of a spouse	100
Divorce	73
Marital separation	65
Imprisonment	63
Death of a close family member	63
Personal injury or illness	53
Marriage	50
Dismissal from work	47
Marital reconciliation	45
Retirement	45
Change in health of family member	44
Pregnancy	40
Sexual difficulties	39
Gain a new family member	39
Business readjustment	39
Change in financial state	38
Death of a close friend	37
Change to different line of work	36
Change in frequency of arguments	35

Major mortgage	32
Foreclosure of mortgage or loan	30
Change in responsibilities at work	29
Child leaving home	29
Trouble with in-laws	29
Outstanding personal achievement	28
Spouse starts or stops work	26
Beginning or end school	26
Change in living conditions	25
Revision of personal habits	24
Trouble with boss	23
Change in working hours or conditions	20
Change in residence	20
Change in schools	20
Change in recreation	19
Change in church activities	19
Change in social activities	18
Minor mortgage or loan	17
Change in sleeping habits	16
Change in number of family reunions	15
Change in eating habits	15
Vacation	13
Major Holiday	12
Minor violation of law	11

Score of 300+: At risk of illness.

Score of 150-299: Risk of illness is moderate (reduced by 30% from the above risk).

Score <150: Only have a slight risk of illness.

LIST OF BIBLICAL REFERENCES
TO WIDOWS (NASB)

Jeremiah 49: 11

"Leave your orphans behind, I will keep them alive; And let your widows trust in Me."

Mark 12: 41-43

41 Jesus sat down opposite the place where the offerings were put and watched the crowd putting their money into the temple treasury. Many rich people threw in large amounts.

42 But a poor widow came and put in two very small copper coins, worth only a few cents.

43 Calling his disciples to him, Jesus said, "Truly I tell you, this poor widow has put more into the treasury than all the others.

44 They all gave out of their wealth; but she, out of her poverty, put in everything — all she had to live on."

Luke 21: 1-4

1 As Jesus looked up, he saw the rich putting their gifts into the temple treasury.

2 He also saw a poor widow put in two very small copper coins.

3 "Truly I tell you," he said, "This poor widow has put in more than all the others.

4 All these people gave their gifts out of their wealth; but she out of her poverty put in all she had to live on."

Acts 9: 36-42

36 Now in Joppa there was a disciple named Tabitha (which translated in Greek is called Dorcas); this woman was abounding with deeds of kindness and charity which she continually did.

37 And it happened at that time that she fell sick and died; and when they had washed her body, they laid it in an upper room.

38 Since Lydda was near Joppa, the disciples, having heard that Peter was there, sent two men to him, imploring him, "Do not delay in coming to us."

39 So Peter arose and went with them. When he arrived, they brought him into the upper room; and all the widows stood beside him, weeping and showing all the tunics and garments that Dorcas used to make while she was with them.

40 But Peter sent them all out and knelt down and prayed, and turning to the body, he said, "Tabitha, arise." And she opened her eyes, and when she saw Peter, she sat up.

41 And he gave her his hand and raised her up; and calling the saints and widows, he presented her alive.

42 It became known all over Joppa, and many believed in the Lord.

James 1: 22-27

22 Do not merely listen to the word, and so deceive yourselves. Do what it says.

23 Anyone who listens to the word but does not do what it says is like someone who looks at his face in a mirror

24 and, after looking at himself, goes away and immediately forgets what he looks like.

25 But whoever looks intently into the perfect law that gives freedom, and continues in it—not forgetting what they have heard, but doing it—they will be blessed in what they do.

26 Those who consider themselves religious and yet do not keep a tight rein on their tongues deceive themselves, and their religion is worthless.

27 Religion that God our Father accepts as pure and faultless is this: to look after orphans and widows in their distress and to keep oneself from being polluted by the world.

Psalm 68: 4-6

4 Sing to God, sing in praise of his name; Lift up a song for Him who rides through the deserts, Whose name is the Lord, and exult before Him.

5 A father of the fatherless and a judge for the widows, Is God in His holy habitation.

6 God makes a home for the lonely; He leads out the prisoners into prosperity. Only the rebellious dwell in a parched land.

Psalm 146: 8- 9

8 The Lord opens the eyes of the blind;

The Lord raises up those who are bowed down;

The Lord loves the righteous;

9 The Lord protects the strangers'

He supports the fatherless and the widow;

But He thwarts the way of the wicked.

1 Kings 17: 7-24

7 Some time later the brook dried up because there had been no rain in the land.

8 Then the word of the Lord came to him:

9 Go at once to Zarephath in the region of Sidon and stay there. I have directed a widow there to supply you with food."

10 So he went to Zarephath. When he came to the town gate, a widow was there gathering sticks. He called to her and asked, "Would you bring me a little water in a jar so I may have a drink?"

11 As she was going to get it, he called, "And bring me, please, a piece of bread."

12 "As surely as the Lord your God lives," she replied, "I don't have any bread—only a handful of flour in a jar and a little olive oil in a jug. I am gathering a few sticks to take home and make a meal for myself and my son, that we may eat it—and die."

13 Elijah said to her, "Don't be afraid. Go home and do as you have said. But first make a small loaf of bread for me from what you have and bring it to me, and then make something for yourself and your son.

14 For this is what the Lord, the God of Israel, says: 'The jar of flour will not be used up and the jug of oil will not run dry until the day the Lord sends rain on the land.' "

15 She went away and did as Elijah had told her. So, there was food every day for Elijah and for the woman and her family.

16 For the jar of flour was not used up and the jug of oil did not run dry, in keeping with the word of the Lord spoken by Elijah.

17 Some time later the son of the woman who owned the house became ill. He grew worse and worse, and finally stopped breathing.

18 She said to Elijah, "What do you have against me, man of God? Did you come to remind me of my sin and kill my son?"

19 "Give me your son," Elijah replied. He took him from her arms, carried him to the upper room where he was staying, and laid him on his bed.

20 Then he cried out to the Lord, "Lord my God, have you brought tragedy even on this widow I am staying with, by causing her son to die?" 21 Then he stretched himself out on the boy three times and cried out to the Lord, "Lord my God, let this boy's life return to him!"

22 The Lord heard Elijah's cry, and the boy's life returned to him, and he lived.

23 Elijah picked up the child and carried him down from the room into the house. He gave him to his mother and said, "Look, your son is alive!"

24 Then the woman said to Elijah, "Now I know that you are a man of God and that the word of the Lord from your mouth is the truth."

2 Kings 4: 1-7

1 The wife of a man from the company of the prophets cried out to Elisha, "Your servant my husband is dead, and you know that he revered the Lord. But now his creditor is coming to take my two boys as his slaves."

2 Elisha replied to her, "How can I help you? Tell me, what do you have in your house?"

"Your servant has nothing there at all," she said, "except a small jar of olive oil."

3 Elisha said, "Go around and ask all your neighbors for empty jars. Don't ask for just a few.

4 Then go inside and shut the door behind you and your sons. Pour oil into all the jars, and as each is filled, put it to one side."

5 She left him and shut the door behind her and her sons. They brought the jars to her and she kept pouring.

6 When all the jars were full, she said to her son, "Bring me another one."

But he replied, "There is not a jar left." Then the oil stopped flowing.

7 She went and told the man of God, and he said, "Go, sell the oil and pay your debts. You and your sons can live on what is left."

Matthew 25: 42-46

42 for I was hungry, and you gave Me nothing to eat; I was thirsty, and you gave Me nothing to drink;

43 I was a stranger, and you did not invite Me in; naked, and you did not clothe Me; sick, and in prison, and you did not visit Me.'

44 Then they themselves also will answer, 'Lord, when did we see You hungry, or thirsty, or a stranger, or naked, or sick, or in prison, and did not take care of You?'

45 Then He will answer them, 'Truly I say to you, to the extent that you did not do it to one of the least of these, you did not do it to Me.'

46 These will go away into eternal punishment, but the righteous into eternal life."

Luke 2: 36-38

36 And there was a prophetess, Anna the daughter of Phanuel, of the tribe of Asher. She was advanced in years, having lived with a husband seven years after her marriage,

37 and then as a widow to the age of eighty-four. And she never left the temple, serving night and day with fastings and prayers.

38 And at that very moment she came up and began giving thanks to God, and continued to speak of Him to all those who were looking for the redemption of Jerusalem.

REFERENCES

Brand, C., & Draper, C.W., & England, A. (Eds.) (2003). Holman illustrated bible dictionary. Nashville, TN: Holman Bible Publishers.

Chambers, O. (1935). My utmost for his highest. Lancashire, UK: Discovery House.

Cordeiro, W. (2008). The divine mentor: Growing your faith as you sit at the feet of the savior. Minneapolis, MN: Bethany House.

Cybersalt Consulting and Communications. (1998-2017). Jericho walls. Retrieved from http://cybersalt.org/cleanjokes/jericho-walls

Elliott, D.B., & Simmons, T. (2011). Marital events of Americans: 2009. Retrieved from https://www.census.gov/prod/2011pubs/acs-13.pdf

IMDb.com, Inc. (1990-2017). The Linkletter show [1952-1970]. Retrieved from http://imdb.com/title/tt0047714/

Kendall, R.T. (2014). Holy fire: A balanced, biblical look at the Holy Spirit's work in our lives. Lake Mary, FL: Charisma House.

Kendall, R.T. (2001). Total forgiveness. Lake Mary, FL: Charisma House.

MacArthur, J. (1986). Caring for widows - CD set. Grace to You. Retrieved from https://www.gty.org/library/sermons-library/54-39/widows-in-the-church-part-4

Stearns, R. (2009). The hole in our gospel: What does God expect of us? Nashville, TN: Thomas Nelson.

Widow's Hope. (2016). These are the statistics. Retrieved from http://www.widowshope.org/first-steps/these-are-the-statistics/

OFFICE OF THE PRESIDENT
BARRY H. COREY

April 16, 2019

Rolland Wright
President and Founder
The Widows Project
3616 Colby Ave #788
Everett, WA 98201

Dear Rolland,

It was great to meet you when I was in the Pacific Northwest last month, and I just wanted to follow up to say how much I appreciate the Kingdom work you are doing with The Widows Project.

When I brought your brochure back to the office and looked over it, I thought of my sister, Bonnie, whose husband of 27 years died suddenly in February. There is such a deep need to minister to grieving spouses, and I admire your response to this "invisible" population for which God mandates special care. I'm proud to count you among Biola alumni, and I'm grateful to see how you are living out Biola's mission to impact the world for Christ.

I wish you all God's best, and may He prepare your heart anew to celebrate the Resurrection this Easter.

Blessings in Christ.

Sincerely,

ABOUT THE AUTHOR

Rolland is the Founder and President of The Widows Project.

He imagines that he is somewhat like a sheep herder. Currently he works as a school bus driver for a local school district in Mukilteo, Washington and shuttles around close to 400 students per day.

When not driving a school bus, he enjoys writing and playing various board or card games. Social engagements are always on the calendar with friends.

His two (2) life verses are, Acts 17:28 "for in Him we live and move and have our being" (TLV) and Colossians 1:18b "that He might come to have first place in everything." (NASB).

He holds a bachelor's degree from Biola University, has a son Chris married to Cindy (2 daughters Chloe & Brenna); 2 daughters, Jennifer married to Nick (son Carter & daughter Kaylee) and Bethany (daughter Brooke). Rolland's parents, celebrated their 67th wedding anniversary in June 2019.

PLEASE RATE MY BOOK

I would be honored if you would take a few moments to rate our book on Amazon.com.

A five-star rating and a short comment ("Very informative!" or "I know at least 3 people who could benefit from this book!") would be much appreciated. I welcome longer, positive comments as well.

If you feel like this book should be rated at three stars or fewer, please hold off posting your comments on Amazon.

Instead, please send your feedback directly to me, so that I could use it to improve the next edition. I'm committed to providing the best value to our readers, and your thoughts can make that possible.

You can reach me at rolland@thewidowsproject.org.

Thank you very much,

Rolland Wright
President & Founder, The Widows Project
http://thewidowsproject.org
Facebook: https://www.facebook.com/thewidowsproject

HEARTFELT GREETING CARDS

Hello Pastors, Friends, Family .....
At the Widows Project our goal is to
uniquely serve the widow and widower
with the love of Jesus.

The packet that you hold in your hand is
designed to help you connect with your
widowed loved one at several important,
and at times forgotten, moments over the
next year.

Moments like their wedding anniversary,
birthday, and holiday times, when absence
will trigger emotio s and memories. When
you don't know what to say, allow The
Widows Project gregtin cards to express
the love and support of your heart.

Sincerely,
The Widows Project

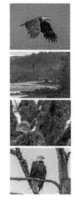

Widow/Widower's name:

Name of loved one who passed:

Address:

Widow Birthday:

Loved one's Birthday:

Wedding Anniversary date:

Date of passing:

Heartfelt Cards
by

Hello Pastors, Friends, Family .....
At the Widows Project our goal is to
uniquely serve the widow and widower
with the love of Jesus.

The packet that you hold in your hand is
designed to help you connect with your
widowed loved one at several important,
and at times forgotten, moments over the
next year.

Moments like their wedding anniversary,
birthday, and holiday times, when absence
will trigger emotio s and memories. When
you don't know what to say, allow The
Widows Project gregtin cards to express
the love and support of your heart.

Sincerely,
The Widows Project

Widow/Widower's name:

Name of loved one who passed:

Address:

Widow Birthday:

Loved one's Birthday:

Wedding Anniversary date:

Date of passing:

Heartfelt Cards
by

If you want to send a card to a widow but don't know what to say, please watch this YouTube video, or take your camera out and point it to the QR code: https://youtu.be/0eOB9baUORQ

Made in the USA
Lexington, KY
13 December 2019

58549218R00077